麦格希 中英双语阅读文库

探险之旅
第1辑

【美】罗莉·波利佐罗斯（Lori Polydoros）●主编
张琳琳　赵子明●译
麦格希中英双语阅读文库编委会●编

全国百佳图书出版单位
吉林出版集团股份有限公司

图书在版编目（CIP）数据

探险之旅. 第1辑 / (美) 罗莉·波利佐罗斯 (Lori Polydoros) 主编；张琳琳, 赵子明译；麦格希中英双语阅读文库编委会编. -- 2版. -- 长春：吉林出版集团股份有限公司, 2018.3（2022.1重印）
（麦格希中英双语阅读文库）
ISBN 978-7-5581-4770-8

Ⅰ.①探… Ⅱ.①罗… ②张… ③赵… ④麦… Ⅲ.①英语—汉语—对照读物②故事—作品集—美国—现代 Ⅳ.①H319.4：Ⅰ

中国版本图书馆CIP数据核字(2018)第046402号

探险之旅　第1辑

编	麦格希中英双语阅读文库编委会
插　画	齐　航　李延霞
责任编辑	欧阳鹏
封面设计	冯冯翼
开　本	660mm×960mm　1/16
字　数	242千字
印　张	10.75
版　次	2018年3月第2版
印　次	2022年1月第2次印刷

出　版	吉林出版集团股份有限公司
发　行	吉林出版集团外语教育有限公司
地　址	长春市福祉大路5788号龙腾国际大厦B座7层
	邮编：130011
电　话	总编办：0431-81629929
	发行部：0431-81629927　0431-81629921(Fax)
印　刷	北京一鑫印务有限责任公司

ISBN 978-7-5581-4770-8　　　　定价：38.00元
版权所有　　侵权必究　　举报电话：0431-81629929

前言 PREFACE

英国思想家培根说过：阅读使人深刻。阅读的真正目的是获取信息，开拓视野和陶冶情操。从语言学习的角度来说，学习语言若没有大量阅读就如隔靴搔痒，因为阅读中的语言是最丰富、最灵活、最具表现力、最符合生活情景的，同时读物中的情节、故事引人入胜，进而能充分调动读者的阅读兴趣，培养读者的文学修养，至此，语言的学习水到渠成。

"麦格希中英双语阅读文库"在世界范围内选材，涉及科普、社会文化、文学名著、传奇故事、成长励志等多个系列，充分满足英语学习者课外阅读之所需，在阅读中学习英语、提高能力。

◎难度适中

本套图书充分照顾读者的英语学习阶段和水平，从读者的阅读兴趣出发，以难易适中的英语语言为立足点，选材精心、编排合理。

◎精品荟萃

本套图书注重经典阅读与实用阅读并举。既包含国内外脍炙人口、耳熟能详的美文，又包含科普、人文、故事、励志类等多学科的精彩文章。

◎功能实用

本套图书充分体现了双语阅读的功能和优势，充分考虑到读者课外阅读的方便，超出核心词表的词汇均出现在使其意义明显的语境之中，并标注释义。

鉴于编者水平有限，凡不周之处，谬误之处，皆欢迎批评教正。

我们真心地希望本套图书承载的文化知识和英语阅读的策略对提高读者的英语著作欣赏水平和英语运用能力有所裨益。

丛书编委会

Contents

Adventures With Abuela
与祖母一起探险 / 1

Adventure on the Amazon River
亚马孙河历险记 / 21

Treasure in the Puget Sound
普吉湾的宝藏 / 49

In Huck's Shoes
成为哈克 / 77

In the Name of Discovery
以发现之名 / 102

Atlantic Crossing
横渡大西洋 / 126

Adventure in Bear Valley
大熊谷历险记 / 145

01

Adventures With Abuela

Special Delivery

It was late afternoon in Kanab, Utah, when Adriana Cruz ran inside. Holding a large envelope, she *exclaimed*, "It's the letter from Abuela!"

Her brother, Rob, looked up from the book he was reading. "Get Mom and Dad!" he said. "They'll want to open it right away."

Their little sister, Emily, put her hands on her *hips*, looking *puzzled*. "Abuela sends us stuff all the time. What's the big deal?"

与祖母一起探险

特殊的信

犹他州,卡纳布市的一个午后,爱祖莲娜·克鲁斯跑进屋子,手里拿着一个大信封喊道:"祖母来信了!"

她那正在看书的弟弟罗伯,抬起头说:"去叫妈妈和爸爸,他们肯定想马上拆开看。"

他们的小妹妹艾米丽叉着腰,看起来很迷惑。"祖母总给我们寄信,这有什么大不了的吗?"

---

exclaim *v.* 惊叫;呼喊　　　　　　　　　　hip *n.* 臀部;髋
puzzled *adj.* 困惑的

ADVENTURE TRIP I

◆ ADVENTURES WITH ABUELA

Adriana explained, "This is a special letter. It contains *clues* to an adventure!"

"Clues?" Emily asked.

"Remember, in her last email Abuela told us she was going to send us clues about our *vacation*," Rob said.

"That's no *mystery*," Emily said. "Mom and Dad already told us we were going to Abuela's house."

"But we have to solve a mystery on the way there," Adriana explained. "And this has the clues."

Their parents walked into the living room. "What's all the *buzz about*?" Mr. Cruz asked.

爱祖莲娜解释说："这是一封特殊的信，里面有探险的线索！"

"线索？"艾米丽问。

"记得吗，她在最后一封电子邮件中告诉我们，她会把假期旅行的线索寄给我们。"罗伯说。

"那不是什么秘密。"艾米丽说，"妈妈和爸爸已经告诉我们了，说我们去祖母家。"

"可是在我们去那儿的路上要解开谜团。" 爱祖莲娜解释道，"这封信里就有解开谜团的线索。"

他们的父母走进客厅。"你们在这叽叽喳喳地干什么呢？"克鲁斯先

---

clue *n.* 线索　　　　　　　　vacation *n.* 假期
mystery *n.* 秘密　　　　　　 buzz about （忙得）团团转

ADVENTURE TRIP I

"The letter from Abuela is here!" the children exclaimed.

"We're leaving Kanab tomorrow so it came just in time," Mrs. Cruz said.

The family *gathered* to read the letter.

Dear family,

*I am taking you on a **wonderful** trip. Let's see if you can **figure out** where we are going. I have sent you clues.*

As you drive, use the clues to try and figure out where we will meet.

*I will give you a **hint**: All the answers to my clues can be found on an Arizona map.*

The clues are found in smaller envelopes. You may open each clue as you

---

gather　*v.*　聚集　　　　　　　　　　wonderful　*adj.*　美妙的；精彩的
figure out　弄明白　　　　　　　　　　hint　*n.*　暗示；提示

solve the one before it. You may now open the first clue.

Good luck, and I hope I am not sitting at the meeting place alone!

Love,
Abuela

CLUE 1: Books and Scrambled Letters

"Look! She included a map." Rob said, *unfolding* it on the coffee table.

"I think these are the clues," Emily said, pointing to a *bunch* of envelopes held together with a rubber band.

Mr. Cruz held up a *sealed* envelope. "We are supposed to open this one first," he said, as he opened the envelope. He pulled out the paper and read:

信封。现在你们可以拆开第一个小信封了。

祝你们好运，希望我不会一个人坐在我们会面的地点！

爱你们的祖母

第一条线索：书和文字的读音

"看呀，她还给了我们一张地图。"鲍勃说着把地图打开放在咖啡桌上。

"我想这些就是线索。"艾米丽指着一扎儿用橡皮筋系在一起的信封说。

克鲁斯先生拿起了一个封着口的信封。"我们应该先拆开这个。"说着打开了信封。他取出一张纸，读道：

---

unfold *v.* （使）展开；打开　　　　　　　　bunch *n.* 束；串；扎
seal *v.* 封上（信封）

ADVENTURE TRIP I

> *Clue 1*
>
> *To begin our vacation game go to the city with a name that tells a common part of each and every book. When you get to the city, "SHOUT!" Then unscramble the letters in shout to tell you which direction to take.*

Emily said, "Let's look at the map. Abuela said all the answers were on the map. If we look at the map maybe we can find a city that is part of a book."

"Hmm," said Adriana, "I think it might be easier to list the parts of a book. I think there are fewer parts of a book than cities in Arizona."

第一个线索

我们行程的第一站是去一个城市，它的名字是每个书籍都有的一个普通的部分。到达那里后，"喊！"然后，"喊"里面的发音会告诉你们行驶的方向。

艾米丽说："我们看看地图。祖母说答案都在地图上。如果我们察看地图，或许可以找到一个以书的组成部分命名的城市。"

"嗯，"爱祖莲娜说，"我想，列出书的组成部分可能会更容易些。书的组成部分要比亚利桑那州的城市少得多。"

---

unscramble *v.* 译出密码；解码

◆ ADVENTURES WITH ABUELA

"Great idea!" exclaimed Rob, and he started making a list. "Let's see, there are *covers*, a table of *contents*, and page numbers…"

"Pages! All books have pages but they might not have a table of contents!" said Adriana.

"Great! Let's see if there is a Pages, Arizona, on the map," said Rob.

"There's not Pages, but there is a Page, Arizona! It is in the northern part of the state, almost in the center," stated Adriana.

"Well, then that is where we will drive tomorrow after we have had a good breakfast," said Mrs. Cruz.

"好主意！"罗伯高声地说，接着开始列书的组成部分。"我们看看，有封皮，目录，还有页码……"

"一定是页码！所有的书都有页码，但不一定全都有目录！" 爱祖莲娜说。

"对！我们来看一下，亚利桑那州的地图上有没有一个叫页码的地方。"罗伯说。

"没找到叫页码的城市，但是亚利桑那州有一个叫书页的地方。它在亚利桑那州的北部，接近中心地带。" 爱祖莲娜说。

"那么，那个地方就是我们明天吃完丰盛的早饭后，将要去的地方。"克鲁斯夫人说。

---

cover n. （书等的）封面　　　　　content n. （书的）目录

ADVENTURE TRIP I

CLUE 2: Names and Paintings

The next morning, an hour after an early breakfast, they *rolled* into Page and gave a loud SHOUT.

"Now we have to figure out what *direction* to go using the letters in the word shout," said Rob.

"Well it shouldn't be west because we just came from there, and Abuela wouldn't send us back in the same direction," said Adriana.

"You *sillies*. It's south! You just move the h to the end," cried Emily.

"Hey, don't we get to open the next clue now that we are in Page?" remembered Dad.

Mom opened the next clue because Dad was driving. Mom read,

第二条线索：名字和图画

第二天早上，吃完早饭一小时后，他们开车到了书页市，然后大声地发出了"喊"。

"现在，我们必须要从'喊'的发音中找出我们要开往的方向。"罗伯说。

"那肯定不是西，因为我们刚从西面来到这里，祖母不会让我们回到西面。"爱祖莲娜说。

"你们真傻。是南边！把字母'h'移到最后。"艾米丽喊道。

"喂，既然我们现在已经在书页市了，现在是不是应该打开下一个信封了？"爸爸想起来。

爸爸在开车，所以妈妈打开了下一个信封。妈妈读道："第二个线

---

roll *v.* 开始移动   direction *n.* 方向
silly *n.* 傻孩子

◆ ADVENTURES WITH ABUELA

"Clue 2. You should be in Page, Arizona and traveling south."

"Yeah!" cheered the Cruz children. "We were right."

Clue 2
*After you Spring along the Ridge and across the Gap, you will get to the exit to a town that thinks it's a city and is often a member of a band. When you get there, start looking for something this picture **represents**. When you are traveling through it, open Clue 3.*

Mom continued reading.

"It's a drawing of a *paintbrush* and a *cactus*," Adriana said, "but

---

索,你们现在应该在亚利桑那州的书页市了,并且在向南开。"

"哇!"克鲁斯家的孩子们欢呼着,"我们猜对了。"

第二个线索

你们喝着泉水一直走到山脊,然后穿过峡谷,你们就会在公路上看到一个通往某个小镇的出口。这个地方你们会以为是一个城市,它的名字常用来表示一种乐器。你们到达那里后,开始寻找这幅图画代表的地方。你们找到那个地方的时候,在路上打开第三个线索。

妈妈接着念。

"这是一幅画着画笔和仙人掌的图画。"爱祖莲娜说,"可它代表什

---

represent *v.* 代表　　　　　　　　　　paintbrush *n.* 画笔
cactus *n.* 仙人掌

ADVENTURE TRIP I

what does it mean?"

"Let's look at the map. I don't see any cactus, and certainly there are no paintbrushes. Read the clue again, Mom," asked Rob.

Mom read the clue again and said, "Oh, I just noticed that Spring, Ridge, and Gap are all *capitalized*. That means they might be the name of something. All place names are capitalized."

Adriana opened the map. "Here it is! Highway 89. We are supposed to drive south on Highway 89!"

"Let me see," said Rob as he *grabbed* the map. "Look Highway 89 goes through Bitter Springs, *Cedar* Ridge, and The Gap—places just like Mom thought."

么意思呢？"

"我们看看地图吧。我没看见任何仙人掌，也一定不会有画笔。妈妈再读一遍吧。"罗伯请求道。

妈妈又读了一遍，然后说："对了，我刚刚注意到泉、脊和谷都是首字母大写的。那就表示，它们可能是地名的一部分。地名一般都是首字母大写。"

爱祖莲娜展开地图。"在这里！89号公路，我们应该沿着89号公路往南开！"

"让我看看。"罗伯说着抢过地图。"看，89号公路经过'苦

---

capitalize *v.* 用大写字母书写；把……首字母大写 grab *v.* 抓住；夺得
cedar *n.* 雪松

◆ ADVENTURES WITH ABUELA

"Good, then 89 must be the right road," said a *relieved* Dad. "What about that town that thinks it's a city and is often a member of a band. *What the heck* does that mean?"

"Hmm," said Rob. "I've got it! It's Tuba City. I see from the map *legend* that Tuba City is really a town, and I know that tubas are *musical instruments* in bands."

CLUE 3: Towns and Flags

Several hours passed as the children searched every billboard, sign, and building along Highway 89 for something that matched the drawing. They had passed the exit to Tuba City and were starting to get nervous.

泉'，'雪松脊'和'大峡谷'——这些地方跟妈妈想的一样。"

"很好，那么89号公路就是我们要走的公路。"爸爸放心地说。"那么我们认为是城市，经常出现在乐队里的那个小镇又是哪儿呢。到底是什么意思呢？"

"哎呀，"罗伯说，"我找到了！是大号市。根据地图图例，大号市实际上是一个小镇，我知道大号是乐队里的乐器。"

第三条线索：小镇和国旗

几个小时过去了，孩子们一直在89号公路沿途的广告板、标志和建筑中寻找图画中的图案。他们已经过了大号市的出口，开始慌张起来。

---

relieved *adj.* 放心的
legend *n.* （地图或书中图表的）图例

what the heck 到底；究竟
musical instrument 乐器

ADVENTURE TRIP I

"Maybe we missed it," said Adriana.

"I don't think so," said Mom, "but just look out of the window. Aren't these rocks beautiful? It's almost as if someone painted them with a *rainbow*."

"Painted with a paintbrush?" asked Emily.

Just then Adriana saw a sign "Painted Desert." "That's it!" she cried. "Emily, you are a genius! Paintbrush and cactus—we are in the Painted Desert. Mom, open the next clue and let's see if we are right!"

"也许我们走过了。" 爱祖莲娜说。

"我想没有。" 妈妈说，"我们看看窗外。这些岩石难道不漂亮吗？就好像是有人用彩虹给它们画上了颜色一样。"

"用画笔画的吗？" 艾米丽问。

就在这时，爱祖莲娜看到了一个标志"红土荒原"。"就是那个地方！" 她喊道："艾米丽，你真是个天才！画笔和仙人掌——我们在红土荒原里。妈妈，看看下一个线索吧，看看我们猜得对不对！"

---

rainbow *n.* 彩虹

Mom read:

Clue 3
You should have passed Bitter Springs, Cedar Ridge, The Gap, and the Tuba City exit. Now you should be traveling along the Painted Desert.

The children all *screamed*, "Yes!"

Mom continued.

> Your great-grandmother *recited* this poem in school when she was a child. When you reach the Arizona city it *reminds* you of, call me on the phone.

妈妈读道:

第三条线索

你们应该已经过了苦泉、雪松脊和大峡谷,还有大号市出口。现在你们应该在红土荒原里。

孩子们齐声喊道:"猜对了!"

妈妈接着念。

你们的曾祖母小时候在学校里,背下了这首诗。你们到达这首诗让你们想到的亚利桑那州这个城市的时候,给我打电话。

---

scream *v.* 尖叫;拼命叫喊　　　　　　　　　　recite *v.* 背诵
remind *v.* 提醒;使想起

ADVENTURE TRIP I

> ### O Flag of Our Union
>
> *O Flag of our union, to you we'll be true, to your red and white stripes, and your stars on the blue; the emblem of freedom, the symbol of right, we children salute you, o flag fair and bright!*

"Oh, man. It's all about a flag. Where are we going to find a flag in the middle of the desert?" *moaned* Rob.

"I've seen flags at gas stations," stated Emily.

"Yeah, but a gas station isn't a city. Abuela said when we get to the city the poem reminds us of, to call her," said Rob.

"I know," said Adriana. "Remember, Abuela also said that all the

---

哦，我们的国旗
哦，我们的国旗，我们真心向你，
你红白的条纹，还有你蓝色的星星；
你是自由的化身，权力的象征，
孩子们敬仰你，哦，公平和快乐的标志！
"哦，天啊。说的都是国旗。我们在茫茫的荒原中，上哪里去找一面旗呢？"罗伯抱怨道。
"我在加油站见到了国旗。"艾米丽说。
"不错，不过加油站不是城市。祖母说我们到达这首诗让我们想到的城市的时候，给她打电话。"罗伯说。
"我知道了。"爱祖莲娜说，"记得吗，祖母也说过这些所有的线索

---

emblem *n.* 象征；标志　　　　　　　　salute *v.* 致敬
moan *v.* 抱怨

clues can be found on the map. Let's look at the map and find the cities. Maybe if we read the city names we can find one that reminds us of a flag. Cities have bigger *dots* on this map than towns."

The children looked for all the cities on the map, Phoenix, Tucson... "FLAGSTAFF!" they shouted. "Dad, quick, drive to Flagstaff!"

CLUE 4: More Letters and Quarters

They drove to a rest stop near Flagstaff, and Dad called Abuela on his cell phone.

"Wow, you have done a great job! I hope you're in Flagstaff," said Abuela over the phone. "Put me on the *speakerphone* so everyone

---

都能在地图上能找到答案。我们看看地图，查查那些城市。也许我们看一下这些城市的名字，就能找到那个跟旗有关的城市。城市在地图上要比镇的标志大。"

孩子们在那张地图上察看所有的城市，凤凰城，图森……"旗杆市！"他们大声喊道，"爸爸，快点，往旗杆市开！"

第四条线索：更多的文字和25美分的硬币

他们来到了旗杆市附近的一个休息站，爸爸用手机给祖母打电话。

"哇，你们做得不错！我希望你们在旗杆市。"祖母在电话那头说，"把电话开免提，这样大家都能听见。"

---

dot *n.* 点   speakerphone *n.* 扬声电话

ADVENTURE TRIP 1

can hear."

 Hi everyone. Here is Clue 4. Unscramble the letters in Clue 3 that chose not to join. Go two hours east on Interstate 40. And meet me at the head of Washington's coin.

 "See you in two hours!" Abuela said.

 "Bye, Abuela!" the children shouted.

 "I guess we need to pull out the map again," said Rob.

 "And don't forget Clue 3," said Emily.

 The children saw that some of the letters were different from the other letters in Clue 3. They *figured* that those were the letters that

---

 嗨，大家好。这是第四个线索。重新排列第三条线索里的文字，在州际40号公路上向东开两个小时。我们在25美分硬币上的华盛顿头上见面。

 "两小时后见！"祖母说。

 "再见，祖母！"孩子们喊道。

 "我想我们需要再把地图打开。"罗伯说。

 "别忘了第三条线索。"艾米丽说。

 孩子们在第三条线索中，看到有一些字母跟其他的字不一样。他们想

---

interstate n. 州际公路   figure v. 认为；推测

◆ ADVENTURES WITH ABUELA

didn't join. But when they listed the letters, F, i, e, t, d, i, P, r, o, e, e, r, s, f, t, they didn't *make sense*.

Then Adriana remembered that Abuela had said to unscramble the letters. So they each played with the letters. They scrambled and unscrambled them as Dad drove.

They had made Peter Fest, and Free Poets but nothing was making sense. Then Dad reminded them of the map.

"We are driving two hours east on I-40. Maybe you can use the scale of miles on the map to figure out how far two hours driving would be and see if something near that *spot* has the letters you listed."

这一些就是不一样的字。但是，把F, i, e, t, d, i, P, r, o, e, e, r, s, f, t, 列出来的时候，看不出来什么。

然后爱祖莲娜想起祖母说要重新排列。于是他们就一起拼这些字母。爸爸开车时，他们仔细地分析研究着。

他们把这两个字连起来，"化石"，"石化"，但都不怎么像。这时，父亲提醒他们看地图。

"我们要在州际40号公路上，向东开两个小时。也许你们能根据里程，在地图上推断出两个小时的车程，看看那附近有没有跟你们重新排列的文字有关的地点。"

---

make sense 有意义；讲得通   spot *n.* 地点

ADVENTURE TRIP 1

F, i, e, t, d, i, P, r, o, e, e, r, s, f, t
fried
Peter
poets
red

"Well, it's about 60 miles from Flagstaff to Winslow," said Rob.

"That means it is about an hour because cars travel about 60 miles an hour. Another hour, or 60 miles from there, puts us at a place called the *Petrified* Forest," said Adriana.

"That's it!" cried Rob. "Abuela is meeting us at the Petrified

"好吧，从旗杆市到温斯罗60英里。"罗伯说。

"那就大约要用一个小时，因为汽车每小时大概行驶60英里。再开一小时，或者说从那儿再开60英里，就会把我们带到一个叫'石化森林'的地方。"爱祖莲娜说。

"就是那儿！"罗伯喊道。"祖母跟我们在石化森林碰面。跟那些字母一样。"

petrified *adj.* （动植物）石化的

◆ ADVENTURES WITH ABUELA

Forest. That has all the right letters."

"But according to this map the forest is huge! How are we going to find Abuela in a forest?" cried Emily.

"She said to meet her at Washington's head," Adriana remembered. "Maybe there's a *statue* there. Wait, didn't she say something about a coin? Washington's head is on a quarter, isn't it?"

"Quarters are even smaller than heads!" cried Rob.

"Well," Mom said, "I believe Abuela's words were 'at the head of Washington's coin.' Perhaps you need to look at the map again."

Adriana read aloud the spots *labeled* inside the Petrified Forest, "Pintado Point, Kachina Point, The Park Headquarters, and

---

"不过，从地图上看，这个森林很大！我们怎么在森林中找到祖母呢？"艾米丽大声问。

"她说我们在华盛顿的头上见面。"爱祖莲娜想起来，"也许那儿有一个雕像。等一下，她是不是提到了什么硬币？25美分上有华盛顿的头像，不是吗？"

"25美分比头还要小，怎么见面呢。"罗伯大声说。

妈妈说："我想祖母说的是'在华盛顿硬币的头上'。也许我们需要再看一下地图。"

爱祖莲娜大声地读出石化森林的景点："马蛟景区、卡其那景区、公园管理处，还有报纸岩。

---

statue *n.* 雕像　　　　　　　　　label *v.* 贴标签于；用标签标明

ADVENTURE TRIP I

Newspaper Rock."

"Wait!" cried Rob. "That's it! The Park Headquarters— we will meet Abuela at the Park Headquarters inside the Petrified Forest!"

Soon the Cruz family pulled into the parking lot at Petrified Forest Park Headquarters. The children *scrambled* out of the car. They found Abuela *cheerfully* talking to a park *ranger*.

"There's my family now," said Abuela. "I thought you'd never get here!"

"Never? That was the shortest drive ever!" said Emily.

"Well, let's go find out about Petrified Forests," said Abuela.

The Cruz family knew they were off on yet another adventure with Abuela.

"等一下！"罗伯大喊。"就是那儿！公园管理处（英语headquarters是由单词头head和25美分quarters）组成。——我们将在石化森林里的公园管理处跟祖母碰面！"

不一会儿，克鲁斯一家开进了石化森林的公园管理处的停车场。孩子们从车里钻出来，他们看到祖母在跟公园管理员愉快地交谈。

"我的家人来了。"祖母说，"我还以为你们永远也找不到这儿呢！"

"永远？我们可一点时间也没耽误！"艾米丽说。

"好吧，我们来看看石化森林里有什么。"祖母说。

克鲁斯一家知道他们又跟着祖母，开始了另外一次探险。

---

scramble *v.* 爬　　　　　　　　　　　　cheerfully *adv.* 愉快地
ranger *n.* 园林管理员

02

Adventure on the Amazon River

Chapter 1: Hammock Life

"Cammy, just try to say it once: 'Obrigada'. It means 'Thank you'."

"Dad, I already told you! I don't speak *Portuguese*, and I don't want to learn."

Cammy's mom *rolled* her eyes. Most of the trip had been like this. For some reason, Cammy was not enjoying the *adventure*. Most

---

亚马孙河历险记

第一章：吊床上的生活

"凯米，再试着说一次：'奥博瑞嘎达'。这句话的意思是：'谢谢你'。"

"爸爸，我已经告诉过你了！我不会说葡萄牙语，我不想学。"

凯米的妈妈无奈地翻了一下眼睛。旅途中的大部分时候都是这样。不知道为什么，凯米不喜欢探险。大多数十二岁的孩子会觉得乘船在亚马孙河上航行，是件非常酷的事。

Portuguese *n.* 葡萄牙语
adventure *n.* 冒险

roll *v.* （使）原地转圈

ADVENTURE TRIP I

twelve year olds would think a boat ride up the Amazon River was pretty cool.

Cammy *poked at* her food. "This is the third lunch in a row they've served this same fish. I'm getting tired of it."

"It's a good thing we brought our own food," said her dad.

"Yeah, but too bad there are ants in our food," continued Cammy. "They climbed right up the poles and into our *stuff*. How did they get on the boat anyway?"

"They must have paid money like the rest of us," *responded* her mom with a smile.

Cammy laughed. "And did the *mosquitoes* pay, too? Because I've got a few bites here on my arm. See?" Cammy held out her tan and bumpy arm. "If I get malaria, I'm holding you two responsible. This

---

凯米拨弄着盘子里的食物:"已经三天了,他们午餐供应的都是这种鱼。我都吃腻了。"

"还好我们有自己带的食物。"爸爸说道。

"可不是嘛,但不幸的是,我们的食物里有蚂蚁。"凯米继续说,"它们顺着柱子一直向上爬,爬进了我们带的食物里。真不知道,它们是怎么上船的呢?"

"它们一定和其他人一样,付了钱才上来的。"妈妈微笑着回答。

凯米笑了。"是不是那些蚊子也付了钱呢?因为它们在我胳膊这已经咬了好几口了。看到了吗?"凯米伸出自己被晒成古铜色的手臂,上面被蚊子叮了好多包。"如果我染上疟疾,你们两个就得负责。因为这次旅行是你们的主意。"

---

poke at (用手指、物件等反复地)捅;扎　　stuff *n.* (泛指的)东西,物品
respond *v.* 回答　　mosquito *n.* 蚊子

trip was your idea."

"Is there anything that you do like about this trip?" her dad asked.

"Let's see . . . that there are only three days left until Manaus? Come on, Dad, you know I like watching the *sunsets*. And yesterday Mom and I saw one of those cool pink dolphins. There! That was pretty positive, eh? Obrigada."

"Well, Ms. *Smarty Pants*," her mom began, "tomorrow we're going to arrive at a town called Santarém. That will be something new to look at."

"Do we get to get off?" Cammy asked.

"No, but you'll get to see an Amazon town up close. And some new people will get on."

"What if I did get off? And *slipped* into the *jungle* and never came

---

"这次旅行中,难道就没有发生什么你喜欢的事吗?"父亲问。

"让我们想想……就是只要再熬三天就能到马瑙斯了?哦,爸爸,你知道我喜欢在船上看晚霞。还有昨天,我和妈妈还看到了一只漂亮的小海豚。对了!还有一件有意义的事,不是吗?奥博瑞嘎达。"

"行了,小机灵鬼!"妈妈开口说:"明天我们就会抵达一个叫圣塔伦的小城。在那儿会有新鲜事发生的。"

"我们下船吗?"凯米问。

"不,但是你将会近距离地观看亚马孙河上游的小城。还会有一些新上船的乘客。"

"如果我下了船,溜进丛林,再也不回来了,会怎么样?"

---

sunset *n.* 晚霞
slip *v.* 溜

smarty pants 自作聪明的人
jungle *n.* 丛林

ADVENTURE TRIP I

back?"

"Then we'd just have to live without you, my dear," said her mom with a smile.

After finishing lunch in the *cafeteria*, Cammy and her parents walked back to their covered sleeping area. They each climbed into their own hammock.

For three days now they had traveled *upriver* on this big boat. Every once in a while they passed little *wooden* houses on the bank of the river, but mostly it was just one thick, green jungle. Cammy reached for her travel *journal* to reread her first three entries.

March 24, 2002

Today we left Canada and landed in a city called Belem. My parents and I are going to travel up the Amazon River in a big three-story boat that

---

"亲爱的！那样的话，我们就只好过着没有你的日子了。"妈妈笑着说。

在自助餐厅吃完午饭后，凯米和父母回到船舱里的睡觉区域。爬上各自的吊床。

到今天，他们的船在亚马孙河上游已经航行三天了。他们偶尔会看到几个在河岸上的小木屋，但大部分时间他们看到的都是郁郁葱葱的丛林。凯米翻看旅行日记，重新看了一遍前三天的日记。

2002年3月24日

今天我们从加拿大出发，坐飞机来到了贝伦市。我和爸爸妈妈要乘坐

---

cafeteria n. 自助餐厅
wooden adj. 木制的

upriver adv. 往上游
journal n. 日记

◆ ADVENTURE ON THE AMAZON RIVER

carries mostly local **Brazilians**. Mom and Dad did it about 20 years ago. (I think they're trying to relive the olden days.) We're going to sleep in big hammocks for six nights!

March 25, 2002

Today was our first day on the boat. My parents are talking to people in Portuguese, and I can't understand anything. I couldn't sleep very well in my hammock. Mom says I'm getting **cranky** already. But nobody here is my age! I wish I was back in Vancouver with my friends. Brian is having a party on Friday, and our soccer team has a **tournament** over the weekend.

March 26, 2002

Today was better. A Brazilian man had a soccer ball, so we played on the top **deck**. It was fun until somebody kicked the ball overboard! Then

---

一艘三层游轮，沿着亚马孙河上游观赏沿途风光。大多数乘客都是巴西当地人。爸爸和妈妈二十年前曾经做过这样的旅行。（我想他们是想重温过去的时光。）我们竟然要在吊床上睡六宿！

2002年3月25日

　　今天是我们第一天上船。爸爸妈妈正在用葡萄牙语跟人聊天，我一点都听不懂。睡在吊床上，我感到很不舒服。妈妈说我变得暴躁了。可是船上连一个跟我同龄的孩子都没有！我真希望自己还在温哥华，跟我的朋友们在一起。周五布莱恩会举办派对，我们的足球队在周末会举行锦标赛。

2002年3月26日

　　今天稍微有点趣。一个巴西人带了一个足球，我们在顶层的甲板上踢了一会儿足球。我们一直玩得很开心，直到一个人把球踢了出去，飞出

Brazilian　n.　巴西人
tournament　n.　锦标赛

cranky　adj.　脾气坏的
deck　n.　甲板

ADVENTURE TRIP I

we sat up top and watched the sun set. It's cool here because you can see forever. And the air here is kind of sweet. Dad says to breathe it in deep now, because it's the best air in the world.

Chapter 2: The Canoe People

On the following day the boat stopped in Santarém, a medium-size town on the bank of the river. A Brazilian family boarded and hung their hammocks in the sleeping area. There was a girl about Cammy's age. She had *curly* black hair and a big smile on her face.

"Hello, do you speak English?" the girl asked Cammy with a foreign *accent*.

"Yes," answered Cammy. "And you are Brazilian? How did you learn English?"

"My family live for one year in Toronto, Canada. So I go to school

---

了甲板。然后，我们就只好站在甲板上看日落。船上的日落很壮观，因为这里视野开阔。亚马孙河上的空气也很清新。爸爸说，深吸一口现在的空气，因为这里的空气是世界上最清新的空气。

第二章：独木舟上的人

第四天，船停在了圣塔伦，一个在河岸边上的中等规模的城镇。一家巴西人上了船，在睡觉区域，挂上了他们的吊床。他家有个跟凯米年龄相仿的小女孩。有一头黑色的卷发，脸上挂着灿烂的笑容。

"你好，你说英语吗？"女孩带着浓烈的地方口音问。

"是的。"凯米回答，"你是巴西人吧？你怎么会说英语？"

"我家在加拿大的多伦多住了一年。所以，我跟加拿大的孩子在一起

---

curly adj. 卷曲的   accent n. 口音

◆ ADVENTURE ON THE AMAZON RIVER

with Canadian kids and learn English. My name is Gabriela."

"Cool. My name is Cammy. It's nice to meet you. Hey, do you want to check out the boat?"

Gabriela smiled. "Yes, sure," she said. "Let's go and see."

The two new friends *explored* the boat from front to back. When they finally reached the top deck, Santarém was already out of sight. As they *gazed* out over the wide river, Cammy spotted two little canoes *paddling* toward the boat. A man was in one canoe and two young boys were in the other. Their skin was dark brown. When they reached the side of the boat, they *slapped* their paddles hard against the water.

"What are they doing?" Cammy asked.

"They are asking for things, like food," Gabriela answered. "It is

---

读书，学习英语。我叫佳波利艾拉。"

"太好了。我叫凯米。很高兴认识你。你想不想去船上逛逛？"

佳波利艾拉微笑着说："当然想，我们现在就去吧。"

这对新朋友走遍了船上的每个角落。最后她们去了顶层的甲板，这时圣塔伦已经消失在视线中了。当她们眺望着开阔的水面时，凯米看到有两个独木舟正向她们的游轮划过来。一只舟上坐着一个男人，另外一只上面有两个小男孩。他们的皮肤是深棕色的，他们靠近游轮的时候，用桨使劲拍打水面。

"他们在干什么？"凯米问。

---

explore *v.* 勘探；探索
paddle *v.* 用桨划船

gaze *v.* 凝视，注视
slap *v.* 拍；打

ADVENTURE TRIP I

kind of like a tradition. Those people are very poor. So the people on these big boats help them out."

Just then somebody from the lower deck threw a white plastic bag into the water. It landed near the two boys. They paddled over to the bag and picked it up before it sank.

Cammy rested her *elbow* on the *railing* and stared out at the canoe family. "I wonder what their lives are like," she said. "Do you think we could make a bag to throw to them?"

"Do you want to?" asked Gabriela.

"Yeah, let's go."

The two girls raced back to Cammy's hammock. Cammy emptied two plastic *grocery* bags and shook out the ants. They quickly filled each bag with fruit, *crackers*, and a can of soda. Cammy also put in a

---

"他们在索要东西，比如食物。" 佳波利艾拉答道，"这已经成了一种习惯。那些人很穷，因此，一些游轮上的乘客会施舍给他们食物。"

就在这时，底下的甲板上有人扔出了一个白色的塑料袋，落在了两个男孩附近。他们向袋子划过去，在它沉入水里之前，把袋子捞了上来。

凯米用胳膊肘倚靠在栏杆上，盯着独木舟上的一家人看。"真不知道他们过着什么样的生活。"她说，"我们也装一袋东西扔给他们怎么样？"

"你想这样做吗？" 佳波利艾拉问。

"是的，我们快点。"

两个女孩跑回凯米的吊床。凯米把两个袋子里的吃的都倒了出来，赶跑了蚂蚁。她们又迅速地向每个袋子里装上了水果、饼干和一瓶苏打水。

---

elbow n. 肘；肘部
grocery n. 食品杂货

railing n. 栏杆
cracker n. 薄脆饼干

◆ ADVENTURE ON THE AMAZON RIVER

bracelet that she had made. Then they ran to the lower deck.

"Hey, look," pointed Gabriela, "there's another canoe coming."

A young boy and an older girl paddled hard to reach the big boat. Then they slapped their paddles against the water and stared up at the two girls.

Cammy and Gabriela threw their bags in close *proximity* to the canoe. The older girl paddled while the young boy *scooped* them *up*. He handed the bags back to the older girl. Cammy could see her pull out the bracelet. She held it in her *palm* and carefully examined it. Cammy *squinted* to see her face, but the canoe had already drifted too far away.

凯米还把自己做的一个手链放进了袋子里。然后，她们朝底层的甲板跑去。

"看，"佳波利艾拉用手指着说，"又过来一只独木舟。"

一个小男孩和一个大一点的女孩向游轮使劲划了过来。然后用桨不停地拍打着水面，抬头盯着凯米她们俩。

凯米和佳波利艾拉尽可能地把袋子扔到独木舟附近。稍大一点的女孩划着桨，小男孩把袋子从水里捞了上来。他把袋子交给女孩。凯米甚至看到她拿出了手链。她把手链放在手中，仔细地看着。凯米眯起眼睛，想要看清她的脸，可独木舟已经走远了。

proximity *n.* 接近
palm *n.* 手掌

scoop up 拿起；捡起
squint *v.* 眯着眼睛看

ADVENTURE TRIP I

Chapter 3: While the Boat Slept

The following day was one that Cammy would never forget. The *swaying* of the hammock somehow woke her up early. She rolled over to see what time it was. The sky was almost totally black, but she could tell that it was dawn. There was a hint of *fuchsia* in the black and a faint *streak* of orange below.

Everyone else was still asleep, rocking quietly back and forth. Cammy's tan feet slipped into her sandals, and she walked up to the top deck.

The air still smelled like fresh rain. Cammy took a slow, deep breath, *inhaling* through her nose. Everything was silent except for the chug and hum of the boat's engine.

The sky grew lighter purple, and Cammy could see where the sun

---

第三章：船上的乘客熟睡时

接下来的一天是凯米永生难忘的一天。摇摇晃晃的吊床很早就把凯米晃醒了。她向舱外看看，想知道几点了。尽管外面还很黑，凯米知道已经到了黎明时分了。天边已经现出一点鱼肚白，底下还透出一点晨光红。

其他人都还在睡梦中，在吊床上摇来摇去。凯米把脚滑入了拖鞋，走上了顶层的甲板。

空气闻起来像清新的雨水的味道。凯米缓缓地吸入一口气，使空气灌入她的鼻腔。河上一片寂静，除了游轮发动机的声音，什么也听不见。

天空渐渐地现出了光亮，凯米看见太阳正在升起。她的目光穿过水

---

sway v. 摇摆
streak n. 条纹；条痕
fuchsia n. 倒挂金钟（灌木，花吊挂，呈红、紫或白色）
inhale v. 吸入；吸气

◆ ADVENTURE ON THE AMAZON RIVER

was going to rise. As she looked across the water toward the trees, she spotted a small person paddling a canoe toward the boat.

Cammy ran downstairs and quietly filled up another plastic bag. Then she ran to the lower deck, but the canoe was still not close enough. Then she climbed to the upper deck. Maybe if she threw it hard enough, the canoe person could reach the bag before it sank.

Cammy stood up on the middle rail and *pressed* her knees into the top rail for support. She *cocked* her arm back, and then *swung* it forward with all of her might. The plastic bag flew out into the river. But Cammy's body leaned too far forward, and her knees *pivoted* over the rail. She fell down, down, down, into the Amazon River.

Cammy's body sank deep underwater. When she finally surfaced,

面，望向树林，她看到了一个小小的人影，坐在独木舟上向游轮这边划过来。

凯米跑到下面的船舱，轻轻地把吃的东西装进了一个塑料袋。然后向底层甲板跑去，可是独木舟离游轮还有点远。然后她爬上了上面的甲板。也许她再使点劲，小舟上的人就能在袋子沉入水中之前，把它捞起来。

凯米站在了围栏中间的栏杆上，用膝盖顶在最上面的栏杆支撑起身体。她把手臂甩到后面，然后使出全身的力气，把袋子抛了出去。塑料袋飞到了河水里。可是凯米的身体倾斜的幅度太大了，膝盖翻过了栏杆。她从船上飞了出去，落到了亚马孙河里。

凯米的身体沉入了水底。当她好不容易浮出水面的时候，游轮已经在

press *v.* 压，挤，推　　　　　　cock *v.* 翘起；竖起（身体某部位）
swing *v.* （使）摆动；摇摆　　　pivot *v.* （使）在枢轴上转动

ADVENTURE TRIP I

the boat was already fifty meters away. "Heeeeelp!" she screamed at the top of her *lungs*. "Somebody help me!"

Cammy *frantically* swam in the direction of the boat. But it continued to *chug* upstream while the current carried her further downstream. Nobody was standing on the decks. Nobody had seen her fall. The sun was not even up yet. The passengers were still asleep in their hammocks.

Chapter 4: The Little River

Cammy felt two hands grab onto her shoulders. Before she knew it, they had pulled her up and into a canoe.

Suddenly she was resting on a huge fish, almost as big as herself. It was cold, *slimy*, and still breathing. "Ahhhhhh!" she screamed, and

---

五十米开外了。"救命！"她拼命地大声叫喊。"有没有人啊！"

凯米奋力地向游轮方向游去。可游轮仍然在向上游行驶，而水流却把她往下游拉。甲板上一个人也没有。没有人看见她落水。太阳还没完全升起，乘客们还在吊床上熟睡。

第四章：小河

凯米感到有两只手抓住了她的肩膀。还没等她反应过来，她就被人从水中捞起，拉到了独木舟上。

她一下子躺在了一条大鱼身上，这条鱼差不多和自己一样大，凉凉

---

lung *n.* 肺
chug *v.* （发动机缓慢运转时）发出突突声
frantically *adv.* 疯狂地；拼命地
slimy *adj.* 黏滑的

◆ ADVENTURE ON THE AMAZON RIVER

jumped away from the fish. A little *giggle* came from the back of the canoe.

Cammy turned around. The canoe's paddler was a little boy no more than eight years old. He had dark brown skin and straight black hair. He wore a red shirt and blue shorts, and his feet were *bare*. The boy stared at Cammy like she was from another planet. Then he looked at the fish and laughed again. Cammy studied him *distrustfully*.

The little boy paddled the canoe toward the shore. There were no houses in sight, but Cammy did spy a narrow *tributary* winding back through the jungle. The boy expertly steered the canoe into that opening, and soon they were traveling deeper into the rainforest.

的，黏糊糊的，还是条活鱼。"啊呀呀！"她大叫着从鱼身上跳了起来。独木舟的后面传来了咯咯的笑声。

凯米转过身，划独木舟的小男孩只有八岁。他有着深棕色的皮肤，黑色的直发。穿着一件红色的衬衫和蓝色的短裤，赤裸着双脚。他愣愣地盯着凯米看，好像在看外星人。之后，他又看看那条鱼，一下子又笑了起来。凯米警惕地打量着他。

小男孩把独木舟划到了岸边。没看见有人家，但是凯米看到一条蜿蜒的小河一直通向丛林。男孩熟练地划入了那片水域，很快他们就驶入了丛林深处。

---

giggle *n.* 咯咯笑
distrustfully *adv.* 不信任地

bare *adj.* 裸露的
tributary *n.* 支流

ADVENTURE TRIP 1

◆ ADVENTURE ON THE AMAZON RIVER

Tree branches and leaves formed a thick green *canopy* overhead. Vines hung down to the water. The little river narrowed. The loudest sound was the light *splashing* of the boy's paddle in the water. Bird and animal chatter echoed throughout the forest like background music.

After another hour of paddling, they arrived at a small house. It was all made of wood: the roof, the walls, the *porch*, and the steps leading down to the little river. There was no glass in the windows and no door on the entrance. They were simply open.

When the little boy shouted up to the house, three kids appeared in the doorway. They stared at Cammy for a moment and then disappeared back inside. She could hear them *whispering* and

---

树枝和树叶浓密地悬在他们头顶上。藤条一直垂落到水面上。河水越来越窄。周围很静，在树林中那些鸟兽的叫声的陪衬下，男孩打在水面上的船桨的声音显得很响亮。

划行了一个小时后，他们来到了一所小房子前。这个房子所有的部分——屋顶、墙壁、前廊以及一直延伸到小河里的楼梯，都是木头的。窗户上没有玻璃，入口也没有门，就这样开放着。

男孩朝屋里喊了一声，在门口出现了三个小孩。他们盯着凯米看了一会儿，就又回到了屋子里。她听到他们在屋里嘀咕着什么，然后就听到了

---

canopy *n.* 天篷似的树荫
porch *n.* 门厅；门廊
splash *v.* 泼洒
whisper *v.* 低声说

ADVENTURE TRIP I

giggling. Finally, a boy in cut-off shorts ran down the stairs and tied up their canoe. He touched Cammy's blond hair and stared at her as if she were an *alien*. Then the two brothers picked up the big fish and quickly ran into the house.

Cammy suddenly felt very afraid. Besides the house, she could not see any other signs of human *existence*. And the jungle was so thick that she could hardly see the sky. A big mosquito landed on her arm and started *sucking* her blood. She slapped at it frantically. "Ahhhh!" Another one landed on her neck. "Malaria!" she screamed, as her hands *spun* like an out-of-control windmill, slapping her body up and down.

咯咯的笑声。最后，一个穿短裤的男孩跑下楼梯，把小舟系在了楼梯上。他用手摸了一下凯米的金色头发，像看外星人一样盯着凯米。这时，他的两个兄弟抬起那条大鱼，很快又跑回了屋子里。

凯米突然间感到很害怕。除了这所房子，她没发现任何人类的迹象。郁郁葱葱的森林里，连天空都看不清楚。一只大蚊子落在了她胳膊上，开始吸她的血。她疯狂地乱拍乱打。"啊呀！"又有一只落在了她的脖子上。她一边喊着"疟疾！"一边挥动着双手，好像一架失去控制的飞机一样，东一下西一下地胡乱拍打着身体。

---

alien *n.* 外星人　　　　　　　　　　existence *n.* 存在
suck *v.* 吮吸　　　　　　　　　　　spin *v.* （使）快速旋转

◆ ADVENTURE ON THE AMAZON RIVER

Giggles came from the direction of the house. Four curious faces *peeked* out of the window. But when Cammy looked up, they ducked down. Their giggles turned into loud laughter.

That's when Cammy started to cry. She lay down on the ground in a ball and sobbed until her whole body *trembled*. Everything was different here, her parents were far away, and these *weird* kids didn't even speak her language. She was lost in the middle of the Amazon rainforest! Cammy closed her eyes and everything went blank.

Chapter 5: The First Night

When Cammy felt a hand on her forehead, the sky was almost completely dark. Rain had started to fall. She could hear it *dripping*

从屋子的方向又传来了咯咯的笑声。从窗户里探出四个小脑袋。但是，当凯米向上看的时候，他们又都把头缩了回去。咯咯的笑声没了，取而代之的是哈哈大笑。

这个时候，凯米哭了起来。她的身体蜷成一团，低声抽泣，浑身发抖。周遭的一切都很陌生，远离父母，那些古怪的孩子也不会说英语。她迷失在了亚马孙河的雨林中了！凯米闭上眼睛，就什么都不知道了。

第五章：第一个夜晚

当凯米感到前额上有一只手的时候，天已经完全黑了，下起了雨。她

---

peek *v.* 微露出；探出
weird *adj.* 奇异的；不寻常的

tremble *v.* 颤抖
drip *v.* 滴下

ADVENTURE TRIP I

through the trees. Cammy's tears had dried, and she was starting to feel cold and wet.

The hand she felt was that of the oldest girl, maybe two years younger than Cammy. Her face was soft and round, with kind eyes that looked like those of an older woman. "Ixtola," she said to Cammy. She put her hand on her chest and repeated, "Ixtola."

Cammy looked up at her and smiled. "Cammy," she said. "I'm Cammy."

Ixtola helped Cammy to her feet and up the wooden steps. On the porch stood a short man with his arms crossed. His eyes studied Cammy distrustfully as she *ducked* under the doorway.

Inside it was dark except for a fire in the middle of the room.

能听到雨点打落在树叶上的声音。凯米脸上的泪水已经干了，她感觉到了寒冷和潮湿。

那只手是那个最大的女孩的，大概要比凯米小两岁。她的脸圆圆的，很温和，像个老妈妈一样慈爱地看着凯米。"埃克斯托拉"她对凯米说。她把手放在自己胸上，反复地说着："埃克斯托拉。"

凯米抬起头看看她，微笑着说："凯米，我叫凯米。"

埃克斯托拉扶起凯米，搀扶着她上了台阶。门廊里站着一个矮个子男人，双手交叉放在胸前。在凯米走进屋子时，警惕地审视着凯米。

除了屋子中间的一堆火外，整个屋子里一片漆黑。木头墙壁上的人影

---

duck *v.* （快速低头或弯腰）躲闪

◆ ADVENTURE ON THE AMAZON RIVER

Shadows danced on the wooden walls. The two boys sat on the floor near the fire. The littlest girl helped a woman *peel* vegetables over a table. That woman had black hair with gray streaks in it. Her eyes were a deep, dark coffee color. She smiled at Cammy and *motioned* for her to sit. Cammy sat on the floor next to her friend, the paddler.

Ixtola's mother handed them bowls containing something white that looked like soup. It had vegetables, leaves, fish, and other stuff in it. There were no spoons. Cammy closed her eyes and took a small sip. "Mmmm," she sighed, opening her eyes. The entire family laughed. They were *relieved* that she liked the food.

After dinner Cammy sipped her tea and watched everyone's

晃来晃去的。两个男孩坐在火堆旁边的地板上，最小的女孩在桌子那头帮一个女人择菜。女人的黑发中夹杂着几根白头发。她的眼睛是深邃的深咖啡色的。她向凯米微笑，并比画着让她坐下。凯米坐在地上，她旁边是那个划桨的男孩。

埃克斯托拉的妈妈递给他们装着白色汤一样东西的饭碗。碗里有蔬菜、树叶、鱼，还有一些其他的东西，没有勺子。凯米闭上眼睛，喝了一小口。"嗯."她很享受地说，并睁开了眼睛。大家都笑了起来。他们看到凯米喜欢他们的食物，松了口气。

晚饭后，凯米一边喝茶一边看着墙上晃动的影子。她顺着飘到窗子

---

peel *v.* 剥皮；去皮   motion *v.* 打手势
relieved *adj.* 放心的

ADVENTURE TRIP I

shadows dance on the walls. She also watched the smoke blow out of the window and into the Amazon sky. "Wow," Cammy thought to herself, "last night I fell asleep next to my parents on the boat. Tonight I'm in the middle of the Amazon, getting fed by *natives*."

Then Cammy slowly looked around the room. The family was softly talking and had stopped staring at her. She took the *opportunity* to study their faces, dirty *fingernails*, and bare feet. These were the kind of *exotic* people that she had only seen on television. But tonight they did not seem very exotic. This was just a family talking after dinner. Each person had a name, just like in Cammy's family.

外面的烟雾，看向了亚马孙的天空。凯米心里想着："昨天晚上我还在船上，睡在父母身边。今天晚上，我就置身在亚马孙的丛林中，接受了土著人的款待。"

然后，凯米看了看屋子里的人。他们一家人在轻声地聊天，没有人注意到凯米。她借着这个机会仔细地审视他们的脸，脏兮兮的手指，还有赤裸的双脚。除了在电视上，凯米从来没见过这样古怪的人。但是今天晚上，他们看起来一点都不古怪。他们只是一户晚饭后聊着天的普通人家。跟凯米的家人一样，也都有自己的名字。

---

native *n.* 土著　　　　　　　　　　opportunity *n.* 机会
fingernail *n.* 手指甲　　　　　　　exotic *adj.* 奇异的

Chapter 6: A World Away

March 30

This was my first full day here. My brain hurts from trying to *communicate* with them. I feel really tired. Last night my body was really *itchy*. I think there are fleas in my bed. And I kept thinking about my parents.

March 31

This morning Ixtola and I went to the garden and pulled up *manioc* roots. In the afternoon we saw a group of little monkeys up close! And then we found some bananas just growing on trees! Ixtola cut them down with her *machete*.

第六章：与世隔绝

3月30日

今天是我感到最充实的一天。跟他们交流让我伤透了脑筋。我感到很疲倦，昨天晚上我浑身痛痒得厉害。我想床上可能有跳蚤。我一直很想念我的父母。

3月31日

今天早上，我和埃克斯托拉去菜园子，拔了一些木薯。下午，我们在附近的树上看到了一群小猴子！然后我们看到了树上的香蕉！埃克斯托拉用砍刀砍下了些香蕉。

---

communicate *v.* 交流　　　　　　　　itchy *adj.* 发痒的
manioc *n.* 木薯　　　　　　　　　　machete *n.* 大刀；大砍刀

ADVENTURE TRIP I

April 1

Today they gave me canoe lessons. Ixtola's dad said to give me one of their canoes to go to Santarém. From there I can get back on a big boat. We can't really talk to each other, but we use our hands until we understand. Ixtola's little brothers taught me how to count *to ten.*

From her favorite tree, Cammy stared down the little river. Tomorrow she would get in the canoe and paddle downstream. She *folded up* the piece of paper that Ixtola had given her and looked back at the wooden house. This place didn't seem so strange anymore. Cammy would miss Ixtola's family, but she *promised* to return. Maybe she would show the rainforest to her own kids someday.

4月1日

今天他们教我学习划独木舟。埃克斯托拉的爸爸说，会把他们的一只独木舟给我，让我划着去圣塔伦。从那里我可以找到可以乘坐的游轮。我们并不能通过语言交流，但是我们可以用手势表达我们的意思。埃克斯托拉的弟弟们教会了我从一数到十。

凯米站在她最喜欢的树上，向下望着那条小河。明天她将划着独木舟向下流去。她折起了一张埃克斯托拉给她的纸，回头看了一眼小木屋。这个地方已经不再那么陌生了。凯米会想念埃克斯托拉一家的，但她也许愿会回来。也许有一天，她会带着自己的孩子来这儿。

---

count *v.* 数数   fold up 折叠
promise *v.* 承诺

◆ ADVENTURE ON THE AMAZON RIVER

Chapter 7: Looking Up

The big boat had reached Manaus, picked up new passengers, and turned around to chug back downstream. Johnnie and Jared were two of its new passengers. Their parents had brought them all the way from Australia to see the Amazon rainforest. They had already slept in hammocks for three nights. The big boat was getting close to Santarém.

"What do you *suppose* their life is like?" Johnnie asked his older brother.

"I don't know," Jared answered, "but they do get to canoe all day. Look, they just grabbed the bag of cookies you threw down!"

Johnnie and Jared watched from the top deck as a little boy with

---

第七章：向上看

那艘游轮已经抵达了玛瑙斯，运载着它的新乘客们，掉转方向，朝下游航行。约翰尼和杰瑞德是其中的两个乘客。他们的父母带他们从澳大利亚来亚马孙热带雨林观光。他们已经在吊床上睡了三宿了。游轮离圣塔伦越来越近了。

"你说他们的生活会是什么样的呢？"约翰尼问哥哥。

"我不知道。"杰瑞德回答，"不过，他们一定整天待在独木舟上。瞧，他们刚刚抓住了你扔出去的装着饼干的袋子。"

当一个棕色皮肤的小孩打开那个塑料袋时，约翰尼和杰瑞德从顶层甲

---

suppose *v.* 认为

ADVENTURE TRIP I

brown skin opened up the plastic bag. "I wonder what kind of house they live in," Johnnie wondered out loud.

"It's *probably* like that small wooden one," said a man who was leaning on the rail.

Johnnie looked over at him and nodded. Next to the man was a woman. She *clutched* a plastic bag in her right hand. "Excuse me, but are you going to throw that too?" Johnnie asked.

The woman looked at him and tried to smile. "Yes, but I'm just waiting for the right moment."

"What's inside?" he asked.

"A wish," she said.

板往下看着。"我真想看看他们住的房子。"约翰尼好奇地大声说。

"也许是一个小木屋。"一个倚在栏杆上的男人说。

约翰尼向他看过去,并点了点头。男人旁边站着一个女人,右手抓着一只塑料袋。"请问,你也打算扔吗?"约翰尼问。

那个女人看了他一眼,努力挤出一个笑容说:"是的,可我正在等待一个合适的时机。"

"里面是什么?"他问。

"一个愿望。"她说。

---

probably *adv.* 可能　　　　　　　　　　　　clutch *v.* 紧握;抓紧

◆ ADVENTURE ON THE AMAZON RIVER

"Hey look, there comes another canoe person now!" Jared *exclaimed*.

From the upper deck they could see a person paddling hard toward the big boat. It looked like a small girl. She slapped her paddle into the water and *waved* her arms.

The woman stood on the middle rail and threw the bag as hard as she could.

The girl paddled to the bag and put it in the canoe. She opened it up and *peered* inside.

Jared looked through his *binoculars*. "That's strange," he said. "It looks like she has blond hair."

"看啊，现在又来了一个划独木舟的人！"杰瑞德高兴地叫着。

站在顶层甲板上，他们能看到一个划独木舟的人，使劲地朝游轮划过来。看起来像个小女孩。她在水中划着桨，舞动着手臂。

那个女人站在中间的栏杆上，使出全身的力气，把袋子扔了出去。

那个女孩向袋子划了过去，把袋子捡到了独木舟上。她打开袋子，向里面翻看。

杰瑞德拿着望远镜。"真怪，"他说，"她好像黄头发。"

---

exclaim *v.* 惊叫；呼喊
peer *v.* 仔细看
wave *v.* 挥动
binoculars *n.* 双筒望远镜

ADVENTURE TRIP I

The man excitedly *tapped* Jared on the shoulder. "Excuse me," he asked, "but can I look through those for a second?"

Jared handed him the binoculars. The man looked through them and started laughing out loud.

"Is it her? Is it her?" the woman asked.

The man laughed again. "It's Cammy alright!" he exclaimed. "You threw that bag down to your very own daughter!"

Something splashed so hard next to Cammy that it almost *tipped* her over. She regained the canoe's balance and looked down into the river.

A man's face slowly *emerged* from the water. "Can you give me a lift, young lady?" he said.

那个男人激动地拍着杰瑞德的肩膀。"打扰一下，"他请求道，"能把望远镜借我一下吗？"

杰瑞德把望远镜递给他。男人拿起望远镜，大声地笑了出来。

"是她吗？是她吗？"女人问。

男人又笑着叫道："正是凯米！你把袋子扔给了自己的女儿！"

有个东西在凯米身边扑打出大片的水花，差点把她打翻。她重新找到了平衡，低头向水中看去。

一张男人的脸慢慢地浮出了水面。"你能带我一程吗，小姐？"他说。

---

tap *v.* 轻拍　　　　　　　　　　　　　　　　　　tip *v.* 倾斜
emerge *v.* 出现

◆ ADVENTURE ON THE AMAZON RIVER

"Dad! What are you doing here?"

"That's what I wanted to ask you," he said, out of breath. "But first help me into the canoe." Cammy pulled her dad up into the canoe and gave him a big, wet hug.

"I fell off the boat. I didn't jump," she wanted to make clear. "But I learned a lot of things."

"Well, I jumped," her dad said. "And I hope it was *worth* it."

Cammy looked up at the big boat as it chugged farther away. She could see her mom waving from the top deck. Cammy waved and blew kisses until she couldn't see her mom anymore.

Then she turned to her dad and said, "It's only about ten hours to Santarém, you know."

"爸爸！你怎么在这儿？"
"这正是我想问你的话。"他气喘吁吁地说。"不过，你最好先把我拉到独木舟里。"凯米把爸爸从水中拉进独木舟里，给了他一个大大的拥抱。
"我是不小心跌下船的，不是自己跳下去的。"她想澄清一下。"不过，我学会了许多东西。"
"我可是自己跳下来的。"爸爸说，"我希望不白跳下来。"
凯米抬起头看到那艘游轮离他们越来越远了。她看到妈妈在顶层甲板上正在挥手，她也不停地挥手向妈妈告别，给妈妈飞吻直到妈妈消失在视线中。
然后，她转身看着父亲说："这儿离圣塔伦只有十个小时的路程。"

worth *adj.* 值得

ADVENTURE TRIP I

"What do you have in the basket?" her dad asked. "Enough food for the both of us?"

"Let's see... I've got bananas, manioc bread, and lots of *mangoes*. There are um, dois, três, quatro, cinco, seis, sete, nove, and dez."

Cammy's dad smiled. "So you could learn a foreign language from natives, but not from your own father, eh?"

"No, Dad. Now I want to learn from you too. Could you teach me to count up to twenty in Portuguese?"

"That depends on how well you canoe, my dear," Cammy's dad said as relaxed his hands behind his head. "This trip was your idea."

"你的篮子里装的是什么？"爸爸问，"够我们两个人吃吗？"

"我们来看一下……我有香蕉、木薯、面包，还有很多忙果。还有……"她用葡萄牙语说出了一连串食物的名字。

凯米的爸爸笑了，"这么说，你跟当地人学了葡萄牙语，而不是从爸爸这学的。"

"不，爸爸。现在，我也想跟你学了。你能教我用葡萄牙语数二十以上的数吗？"

"宝贝，那得看你船划得怎么样。"凯米的爸爸把手放在头下说，"这次旅行可是你的主意。"

---

mango *n.* 杧果

Treasure in the Puget Sound

Chapter One

My name is Tim Hawkins. My friends suggested that I record the story of the *treasure* on an island in the Puget Sound. My friends want the *entire* story to be told, but there is one thing I can't *reveal*. I can't tell you where the island is because there are still riches on that island.

The adventure began when Johnny Bones came to stay at the

普吉湾的宝藏

第一章

我叫蒂姆·霍金斯。朋友们都建议我把普吉湾岛屿上宝藏的故事写出来。他们让我毫无隐瞒地讲出一切,但有一件事我不能讲。我不能告诉你们那个岛屿的具体位置,因为岛上还有大量的钱财。

这次历险是从约翰尼·伯恩斯入住路易斯—克拉克旅馆开始的。我的

---

treasure *n.* 宝藏   entire *adj.* 全部的
reveal *v.* 透露

ADVENTURE TRIP I

Lewis & Clark Inn. My parents owned the inn, and I worked for them.

Bones was a large man with a *hideous* knife scar across his cheek. He was an old seaman and looked the part. Bones *swaggered* into the inn, placed $200 on the counter, and demanded a room. That was an *awful* lot of money when I was a kid, so my father gave him a room without question. Bones dragged his sailor's chest upstairs and settled in.

Most days Bones was quiet and remained in his room, but in the evenings he came downstairs to drink rum. After a few drinks, he got loud and swore. A couple more drinks and he sang old, *vulgar* sailing songs.

Nobody was willing to confront Bones and request that he be more civil. One night he kicked over a chair and Dr. Living, my dad's

---

父母经营着这家旅馆，而我就在那里帮忙。

伯恩斯身材高大，有一条横穿脸颊的难看的刀疤。他是个老水手，还是个小头目。伯恩斯摇摇晃晃地走进旅馆，在前台扔下了二百美元，要开个房间。我当时还很小，在我眼中，这是很大一笔钱。因此，父亲问也没问就给了他一间房。伯恩斯拖着他的水手箱上了楼，住了进去。

白天，他大多数时候都静静地待在房间里，可是到了晚上，他就会下楼喝朗姆酒。几杯酒下肚，他就会大声叫骂。再喝上一两杯，就会唱起那些老水手们经常唱的低俗的歌曲。

没有人敢出面制止伯恩斯，让他自重。一天晚上，他踢翻了一把椅

---

hideous *adj.* 十分丑陋的　　　　　swagger *v.* 摇摇晃晃地走
awful *adj.* 很多的；非常的　　　　vulgar *adj.* 粗俗的

best friend, got angry and told Bones to shut up.

Bones stared Dr. Living in the eye, and Dr. Living stared right back. I thought they were going to fight, but Bones turned and walked away without saying a word. Dr. Living suggested Bones might stop drinking so much rum before the drink killed him.

Chapter Two

After Bones had been living in the inn a few weeks, he hired me to be his *lookout*. If I ever spotted a one-legged man coming toward the inn, he wanted me to *alert* him. Bones seemed very afraid of the one-legged man, so I was curious. It seemed like a *harmless* adventure. I told him I would do it.

Ignoring the doctor, Bones continued drinking rum every night. When I asked why he didn't listen to the doctor, he said he'd get sick

---

子，惹怒了父亲最好的朋友李医生，他喝止了伯恩斯。

伯恩斯死死地盯着李医生的眼睛，李医生也瞪着他。我以为他们会打起来，但是伯恩斯什么也没说，转身离开了。李医生劝他少喝点酒，否则会送命的。

第二章

伯恩斯在旅馆住了几周后，雇我为他放哨。他吩咐我如果看见有一条腿的男人来到旅馆，一定要立即告诉他。伯恩斯似乎很怕这个一条腿的人，所以我感到很好奇。这个任务好像没什么危险，我就答应了下来。

伯恩斯每天晚上还是照旧喝朗姆酒，根本不把医生的劝告放在心上。我问他为什么不听医生的劝告，他说没有朗姆酒，他就会生病。如果你来

---

lookout *n.* 观察员
harmless *adj.* 无害的

alert *v.* 向……报警

ADVENTURE TRIP I

without his rum. If you asked me, he already looked sick.

One night when Bones was drinking and singing, a pale, short man came to the inn. He was dirty and looked like he had just returned from a long *voyage*. That was common. But this man was missing two fingers on his left hand and walked with a *limp*.

When the man saw Bones, he went straight at him. Bones turned and saw him. "Black Dog!" Bones exclaimed. "What are you doing here?"

"I have come for what is owed me," Black Dog replied. He seemed ready to kill to get whatever it was he wanted.

"I have nothing," Bones said. He took a couple of steps backward, seeming a little less *tough* right then.

问我，我会告诉你他看起来已经生病了。

一天晚上，当伯恩斯又喝着酒唱歌的时候，一个面容苍白的矮个男人走进了旅馆。他满身灰尘，看样子刚从海上航行归来。这是很常见的。可是，他的左手少了两根手指，走起路来还一瘸一拐的。

当他一看到伯恩斯，就径直朝他走过去。伯恩斯转身看到了他。"黑狗！"伯恩斯喊道，"你来这做什么？"

"我来要回属于我的东西。"黑狗答道。他好像随时准备为要回他的东西跟人拼命。

"我没拿。"伯恩斯向后退了几步，少了几分平日里的嚣张。

---

voyage n. 航海　　　　　　　　　　　　limp n. 跛行
tough adj. 强硬的

◆ TREASURE IN THE PUGET SOUND

"Where is it?" Black Dog demanded. He pulled a long, *shimmering* knife from his jacket.

Customers began to *scatter* toward the walls. I was shaking. This was more adventure than I wanted.

"Leave me alone." Bones pulled his own knife. They stared at each other for what seemed like hours.

Suddenly, Black Dog jumped at Bones and *slashed* him on the arm. They *wrestled* for a few minutes, breaking tables and chairs. The rest of us edged toward the door.

Black Dog appeared to maintain the advantage. Then the fight stopped. Suddenly, everything was quiet and no one moved. Black Dog pulled his knife from Bones's chest and wiped the blade on

"东西在哪儿？"黑狗问。他从衣服里掏出一把寒光闪闪的长刀。

客人们吓得一下子都退到了墙边。我也吓得直哆嗦。我可不想经历这样危险的场面。

"别过来。"伯恩斯拔出刀，他们就僵在那里，盯着对方的眼睛。时间好像都凝固了。

突然，黑狗朝伯恩斯扑过去，抓住了他的手臂。他们在一起扭打了几分钟，摔烂了桌椅。我们都想挤出去。

黑狗看起来占了上风。这时，他俩都不动了，不打了。突然间，一切都静止了，大家都一动不动地站在那里。黑狗从伯恩斯的胸膛中拔出刀，

| shimmer *v.* 闪烁 | scatter *v.* 散开 |
| slash *v.* 砍 | wrestle *v.* 摔跤 |

ADVENTURE TRIP I

Bones's *shirtsleeve*.

Chapter Three

Black Dog left Bones and went upstairs. I heard him going room to room, *kicking* in doors as he looked for the room that was Bones's.

Just then, Dr. Living arrived. He went to Bones immediately, but the old seaman was already dead. I explained what had happened and told him Black Dog was still upstairs. After the doctor called the police, I followed him upstairs.

We found Black Dog trying to *pry* open the lock on Bones's chest. When the doctor kicked Black Dog in the back, sending him *sprawling*, the knife slid under the bed. Black Dog got to his feet and the doctor told him to give up, that the police were on their way.

Black Dog had no desire to talk to the police. He ran to the

用伯恩斯的衬衫袖子擦了擦刀刃。

第三章

黑狗撇下伯恩斯，上了楼。我听到他一间一间地踢开房门，寻找伯恩斯的房间。

就在这时，李医生来了。他立刻来到伯恩斯身旁，但是这个老水手已经断气了。我向他解释了发生的一切，并告诉他黑狗还在楼上。医生打电话报了警，我便跟着他上了楼。

我们看到黑狗正在撬伯恩斯箱子上的锁。医生一脚踢在了他身上，他趴在了地上，刀子掉到了床底下。黑狗挣扎着站了起来，医生劝他放弃抵抗，警察已经在来这儿的路上了。

黑狗一点儿也不想见到警察，他跑向窗子，爬下防火梯，逃走了。

---

shirtsleeve *n.* 衬衫的袖子   kick *v.* 踢
pry *v.* 撬开   sprawl *v.* 伸开四肢坐（或躺）

window and climbed down the fire escape.

The doctor finished opening the chest. It was filled with some clothes, an old compass, two *pistols*, and a birth *certificate*. Under that layer was a false bottom. There was some money in the bottom of the chest, all brand-new-looking, and some papers. Among the papers was a handmade map with three red crosses drawn on an island.

Chapter Four

In the packet with the map was a slip of paper with the name Captain Glint written on it. There were also badly written notes that suggested a huge treasure of money might be hidden on the island shown on the map.

Dr. Living thought we should take what we knew to Robert Jacks.

医生接着打开了箱子。里面装着几件衣服，一个旧罗盘，两把手枪，还有一张出生证明。在这些东西下面，有一个暗格。里面是一些新钱和几张纸。纸中间夹着一张手绘地图，地图上的一个小岛上画了三个红色的十字。

第四章

跟地图放在一起的是一张纸，上面写了一个名字"格林特船长"，还有几行潦草的字。看起来好像地图上的那个小岛，很有可能藏有大批宝藏。

李医生认为我们应该把了解的情况告诉给罗伯特·杰克斯。他是一名

---

pistol *n.* 手枪　　　　　　　　　　certificate *n.* 证明

ADVENTURE TRIP I

He was an older, retired fishing captain. If anyone might know about the island on the map, it would be Jacks. We took the map and notes to him, and I *related* as much as I knew about the map and about Bones. I also told him about the one-legged man.

Jacks knew the story. And he knew all about Captain Glint. He believed that if the map was real, there could be a lot of money buried there. The reward would be large.

During World War II, Glint and his men were able to *hijack* a military ship carrying *payroll* for 10,000 soldiers and officers. The ship was outfitted like a fishing vessel so that it wouldn't attract attention. It wasn't well armed and there weren't many gunboats to guard it because of the war. The Navy thought they could *sneak* it into the naval base at Bremerton. Somehow, Glint and his men found out

---

见多识广，退休在家的渔船船长。杰克斯是最有可能知道小岛位置的人。我们把地图和笔记都带给了他，我把知道的关于伯恩斯和地图的所有信息都告诉给了他。我还对他说了独腿人的事。

杰克斯听说过这件事。他知道格林特船长所有的事。他确信，如果这张地图是真的，那么岛上一定埋了很多钱，而且会是一大笔钱。

二战期间，格林特船长和他的手下劫持了一艘军舰，运载着一万名官兵的军饷。为了掩人耳目，这艘军舰伪装成渔船。因为是战争期间，船上没有太多的武装人员，也没有太多的炮舰护航。海军以为他们能偷偷开进

---

relate *v.* 叙述；讲述
payroll *n.* 工资总支出

hijack *v.* 劫持
sneak *v.* 溜

◆ TREASURE IN THE PUGET SOUND

about it and planned an attack.

Glint and his men got away with the payroll and hid the money before they were caught. Most of them got away. Glint was put in prison, where he was killed. During the *trial*, or after, he never *revealed* the location of the buried money.

Chapter Five

After hearing about Bones and the one-legged man, Jacks believed the map was real. He said he would personally find a *crew* to search for the money. He thought he knew the island in the drawing. On the condition that I could serve as *cabin* boy, Dr. Living agreed to let Jacks plan the voyage. The doctor wanted me to have a share of the reward, thinking it might help repair the damage to my parents' inn.

布雷默顿的海军基地。格林特船长和手下不知从哪儿得到了消息，策划了这起事件。

格林特和手下卷走了那批军饷，并在被捕前把钱藏了起来。大多数人都逃走了。格林特锒铛入狱，死在了牢里。他在审讯中从未泄露埋钱的地点。

第五章

听完了伯恩斯和独腿人的事后，杰克斯确信这张地图是真的。他说会亲自带一队人马去搜寻那笔钱。他觉得能找到地图上的小岛。李医生同意让杰克斯去寻找宝藏，条件是让我上船做杂役。医生想让我分到一部分钱，好补偿我父母旅馆的损失。

---

trial *n.* 审判
crew *n.* 一伙人

reveal *v.* 透露
cabin *n.* （轮船上工作或生活的）隔间

ADVENTURE TRIP I

I was excited. It's every boy's dream to go on a voyage searching for buried treasure. I couldn't have asked for a better adventure.

When I got home, the police were just leaving. They asked me what I knew. I was afraid to *lie* to them, but I knew I had to keep the money a secret. As my stomach filled with butterflies, I told them I knew nothing. I hate to tell lies.

Two days later, a boy my age named Frank came to the inn. Frank told me to say goodbye to my parents and meet the Spokane, the boat we would be sailing on, down at the fisherman's *terminal* on the docks. Jacks sent Frank to work for my parents while I was gone.

This was the first time I'd ever left home, and I was sad to say goodbye to my mom. I have to *admit* I cried a bit. As excited as I was, I was also afraid. I ran all the way to the *waterfront*.

我很兴奋，出海航行寻找宝藏是每个男孩梦寐以求的事情。这是我最大的梦想。

我回到家时，警察正要离开。他们向我了解情况。我很害怕，对他们说谎，我知道决不能泄露那笔钱的秘密。我忐忑不安地对他们说我什么都不知道。我讨厌说谎。

两天后，一个跟我差不多大的男孩弗兰克来到了旅馆。他让我跟父母告别，出发去找斯伯坎号，就是那艘寻宝船。它现在就停在渔船停放的码头。弗兰克是杰克斯派来的，我出海期间，他代替我在旅馆帮忙。

这是我第一次离开家，跟妈妈道别时，我很难过。我得承认，我当时

---

lie *v.* 撒谎
admit *v.* 承认

terminal *n.* 终点站
waterfront *n.* 码头区

◆ TREASURE IN THE PUGET SOUND

Chapter Six

When I got to the boat, Captain Elliott welcomed me aboard the Spokane. He told me to report to Old John Gold in the *galley*. Gold was a tall man, missing his left leg from the hip down, and with a green parrot on his shoulder. He had a wooden leg and used a *crutch* to get around.

Gold looked like the man Bones had been afraid would find him. I was shaking a bit when he reached to shake my hand.

"John Gold's the name, ship's cook."

"Tim Hawkins," I replied, still shaking.

"Well, you look fit for an adventure. I hear we are sailing to find some silver." Gold seemed to know more than he should about the voyage. Jacks was supposed to keep the money a secret.

哭了。兴奋的同时，我也有点害怕。我一路跑到海边。

第六章

上了船，我看到艾略特船长站在甲板上迎接我。他告诉我去厨房找约翰·金报到。金个子很高，左腿从臀部以下都没有了，肩上站着一只绿鹦鹉。他装了一条木腿，走路时拄着拐。

金看起来很像伯恩斯害怕的那个人。他过来和我握手的时候，我吓得一激灵。

"我是船上的厨师约翰·金。"

"蒂姆·霍金斯。"介绍自己时我仍然在发抖。

"你看起来很适合去探险。我听说我们是去寻找一批银币。作为一个厨师，金似乎对这次航行太过关心了。杰克斯不应该对别人说钱的事。

---

galley *n.* 桨帆船   crutch *n.* 腋杖；拐杖

ADVENTURE TRIP I

"I wouldn't know," I replied. "I'm just the cabin boy." I hate lying.

John Gold was a strange man, but he didn't seem to be the *ruthless* pirate that Bones thought he was. I couldn't imagine Jacks would hire a pirate as ship's cook, so maybe it wasn't the same man.

Chapter Seven

Captain Elliott didn't like the crew—any of them. He also didn't like that we were sailing to an island based on a handmade map and looking for buried government money. He thought the whole thing was a *foolish* plan.

Jacks *protested* that he didn't tell anyone about the mission, but the doctor and I ignored his *defense*. Dr. Living agreed that the crew seemed untrustworthy. He believed the captain and John Gold were the only honest men on the ship.

"我不了解。"我回答,"我只是个打杂的。"我讨厌说谎。

约翰·金的确是个怪人,可他看起来并不像伯恩斯口中的那个凶残的海盗。我想杰克斯也不会让海盗到船上做厨师,所以也许他不是伯恩斯说的那个人。

第七章

艾略特船长不喜欢这些船员———一个也不喜欢。他也不愿意领我们出海,按照一张手绘地图,寻找埋藏着政府军饷的小岛。他认为整件事都很荒唐。

杰克斯向我们保证他没告诉任何人宝藏的事,但我和医生都不相信他的话。李医生也认为这些船员都不可靠。他觉得在这艘船上只有船长和约翰·金是可靠的。

---

ruthless *adj.* 残忍的
protest *v.* 声明;申明

foolish *adj.* 愚蠢的
defense *n.* 辩解

◆ TREASURE IN THE PUGET SOUND

Too many of the crew had guns for me to feel safe, and I only trusted the doctor and the captain. Maybe John Gold was a good man, but I didn't understand why he would leave his own *pub* behind to be a cook on a ship. He had to know something about the money.

The captain agreed to stay on board and lead the voyage, but he brought a few of his own men as part of the crew. I *suspected* we might need some friends when we reached the island.

Chapter Eight

The voyage to the island took only a few hours. Between Jacks and the captain, there was no problem reading the map. There were so many islands in the Puget Sound, it *confounds* me how anyone could tell one from another.

那些船员们都带着枪，这让我觉得很不安全。我只信任医生和船长。也许约翰·金是个好人，可我不明白他为什么会放下自己的酒馆，来这条船上做厨师。他一定知道这笔钱的事。

船长同意留在船上，领我们出海航行。但他坚持带了一些自己人上船。我想，到了岛上，我们也许会需要一些帮手。

第八章

我们只在海上航行了几个小时，就抵达了目的地。杰克斯和船长很擅长看地图。在普吉湾有这么多的岛屿，真不知道人们是怎么区分它们的。

---

pub *n.* 酒馆
confound *v.* 使困惑

suspect *v.* 怀疑

ADVENTURE TRIP I

We dropped anchor just off shore from a large island covered with forest. When Jacks told the captain to pull into a small *cove* with a sandy beach, I could feel my heart race. This was it—we had found the island.

It was late in the day, so a thorough search of each possible site wouldn't begin until the morning. For now, everyone wanted a place to sleep. I found an old apple *barrel* on deck and climbed inside to get out of the wind that seemed to never stop blowing.

As I got settled to sleep a bit, I *overheard* Gold and some of the crew talking nearby. What I heard frightened me. I became *convinced* that the lives of all the honest men on board were in danger.

John Gold's words were terrifying. He had served under Captain Glint and called himself a "man of opportunity." I assumed this

---

我们在一个森林覆盖的大岛岸边抛下了锚。当杰克斯让船长把船驶入一个有着沙滩的小海湾时，我的心激动地怦怦直跳。这就是我们寻找的那个岛屿。

天色已晚，所以要等到天亮，才能开始彻底地搜寻每个可能的地点。现在，大家能做的就是找地方睡觉。我在甲板上发现了一个苹果桶，钻了进去。这样，不停地刮着的海风就吹不到我了。

我刚刚有点睡意时，就无意中听到了在附近的金和一些船员的谈话。他们的话把我吓坏了。我很确定船上的那些老实人有生命危险了。

约翰·金的话很可怕。他曾经是格林特船长的手下，自称为"幸运

---

cove　*n.*　小海湾　　　　　　　　　　barrel　*n.*　桶
overhear　*v.*　偶然听到　　　　　　　convinced　*adj.*　确信的

meant he was a pirate and a killer. The plan, as he explained it, was to wait until the doctor and Jacks *discovered* the money and *loaded* it onto the ship. Once we were heading toward home, he and his men would *mutiny* and commandeer the ship. All those who opposed him would be killed.

I was very afraid. Gold explained the details of his plan to his men. Then, suddenly, he told one of the sailors to see if there were any apples in the barrel. I *panicked* and just before he reached into the barrel, another of the men suggested they drink to seal their plan. Agreeing enthusiastically, they all went to get their rum. I jumped from the barrel and ran to the find the doctor.

Chapter Nine

I explained to the doctor and captain what I had overheard, and

---

星"。我断定这意味着他是海盗，是杀人犯。按照他的讲述，他的计划是等着医生和杰克斯找到那些钱，把钱运到船上。一旦我们返航回家，他和同伙就发动叛乱，占领船。把反抗的人都杀死。

我非常害怕。金向同伙详细地解释着他的计划。这时，他突然让一个水手看看桶里有没有苹果。我很惊慌，就在他要把手伸进来时，另外一个水手提议喝酒庆祝一下他们的计划。这些人都迫不及待地同意了，都去找朗姆酒了。我从桶里跳出来，跑去找医生。

第九章

我把无意中听到的话告诉给医生和船长，他们也都觉得我们的处境很

---

discover *v.* 发现
mutiny *v.* 哗变；暴动
load *v.* 装上
panic *v.* 惊慌失措

ADVENTURE TRIP I

they agreed that we were in danger. The captain suggested we should continue with the mission. If we stopped now, he thought, Gold would stage a mutiny and kill us immediately. We would wait for the right moment and *launch* our own attack.

The following morning was, as usual, cold and rainy. I was feeling a touch of *seasickness*, so I skipped breakfast. I went to the island with the captain and the doctor. As soon as we reached shore, I *slipped* away on my own because I didn't want to be around Gold and the other men any longer.

As I explored the island, I found the foliage thick and the ground rough. After an hour or so, I was standing in a clearing not far from a *creek* that ran down to a beach. For the first time since I heard Gold and his men discussing their plan, I felt excited again. I experienced

---

危险。船长建议我们继续寻找宝藏。如果我们现在停下来，金就会发动叛乱，立即杀掉我们。我们应该等待合适的时机，发起攻击。

第二天早上，跟平时一样，下起了雨，冷飕飕的。我有点晕船，所以没吃早餐。我跟着医生和船长去了小岛。一上岸，我就自己走开了。因为我再也不想跟金和他的同伙待在一起了。

在岛上闲逛时，我发现岛上的地面很硬，上面还覆盖着厚厚的落叶。大约一个小时后我站在小溪旁边的空地上。这条小溪通向岸边。自从听到

---

launch *v.* 发起
slip *v.* 悄悄疾行

seasickness *n.* 晕船
creek *n.* 小河；小溪

◆ TREASURE IN THE PUGET SOUND

the *thrill* of exploration as I heard wild birds and strange noises I couldn't identify.

While I stood in the clearing, I saw something moving just beyond the trees. I had no idea what kind of animals might live on this island. Given the choice, I'd rather go back to the search group. At least with Gold, I knew what I was up against.

As I walked, the creature seemed to move very *swiftly* from tree to tree, as though it was trying to head me off. I pulled my knife from my belt, hoping to *defend* myself as best I could. To my surprise, the creature leapt from the trees and threw itself at my feet. It was a man.

He begged to be taken from the island. He said his name was Ron Gunn and that he had been *stranded* for many years. Dressed

---

金和同伙讨论他们的计划后，我第一次感到那种兴奋又回来了。听着那些野鸟的叫声和不知道的声音，我有了探险的冲动。

站在空地上时，我看见树林那边有东西在动，我不知道岛上会有什么样的动物。可以的话，我宁愿回去跟他们一起寻找宝藏，至少跟金在一起，我知道敌人是谁。

我走动时，那个东西在树丛中动得更快了，好像打算追上我。我从腰间拔出刀，想拼死一搏。令我惊讶的是，那个东西从树林中窜了出来，跳到了我的脚边。竟然是个人。

他乞求我带他离开小岛。他说自己叫罗恩·甘，已经在岛上待了很多

---

thrill *n.* 兴奋　　　　　　　　　　swiftly *adv.* 迅速地
defend *v.* 保护　　　　　　　　　 strand *v.* 使滞留

ADVENTURE TRIP I

in old *rags*, he was very *tan* and dirty. He said he was a member of Glint's crew who had been left behind when he disagreed with their plans for the money. I told him some of Glint's men were on the island now.

Gunn knew the island well, and he knew where the money was buried. He thought for a minute and decided he had a plan, but he needed to know if there were any crewmen who were not with Gold. I said there were at least ten honest sailors, including Gunn.

Chapter Ten

While the rest of the crew searched for *landmarks* that might lead to the red crosses on the map, we dug the money from its hiding place. Gunn said two of the crosses were false marks—that only one cross was the true location where the money was buried. We pulled

---

年了。他穿得破旧不堪，皮肤黝黑，浑身上下脏兮兮的。他曾经是格林特的船员。因为反对抢劫那笔钱被留在了岛上。我告诉他，格林特的一些手下现在就在岛上。

甘对这个小岛很熟悉，也知道埋钱的地点。他想了一会儿，有了对策。他想知道除了金和他的手下，还有多少可靠的水手。我说包括甘在内，至少有十个。

第十章

就在其他船员寻找路标，想通过路标找到地图上画十字的地方的时候，我们把钱挖了出来。甘说其中有两个十字标记是假的——只有一个十

---

rag *n.* 破布　　　　　　　　　　　tan *adj.* 棕黄色；棕褐色的
landmark *n.* 路标

◆ TREASURE IN THE PUGET SOUND

twenty boxes of money from the hole and then put the dirt back. After Gunn hid his *shovel*, we moved the money to a shallow cave he had dug into a small mountain on the island.

There was a lot of money in those boxes, easily more than a million dollars. That's not an amazing amount of money today, but back then it was a fortune. *Scoundrels* would do anything to get their hands on that much money.

Gunn figured they would *split* up to search for the money. When one of the smaller groups found the actual spot, we would try to split them up. While we waited, I felt more and more afraid. Gunn's plan didn't seem too *intelligent* to me.

It seemed like hours had passed before a group of seven men found the hole we had dug. Three of them were the captain's men,

---

字标的是真正的藏钱地点。我们从一个大洞里拖出了二十个装钱的箱子，又把土填了回去。甘藏好了铁锹，我们就把钱运到了之前挖好的小洞里。这个洞在岛上的一座小山下。

那些箱子里有好多钱，一定超过一百万。这些钱在今天也许不算什么，但在那个时候可是一大笔财富，足以令那些恶棍不择手段。

甘猜想他们会分头寻找宝藏。当其中的一队人马找到了真正的藏钱地点时，我们就尽量使他们分开。等待的时候，我越来越害怕。我觉得甘的计划不够智慧。

过了好久，一支七名船员组成的寻宝小队发现了我们挖的洞。其中有

---

shovel *n.* 铁锹
split *v.* 分开
scoundrel *n.* 无赖；恶棍
intelligent *adj.* 聪明的

ADVENTURE TRIP 1

◆ TREASURE IN THE PUGET SOUND

which made me feel a little better. We threw rocks at them and they *scattered* to avoid getting hit. While Gunn stayed hidden, I ran toward the men that I trusted. Gunn continued throwing rocks at Gold's men.

I told the captain's men what was happening. They each had pistols, so we surrounded the others and *confronted* them. They *surrendered* and begged us not to kill them. Gunn helped us tie them up, then we stuffed their shirtsleeves in their mouths. We left them secured to a tree.

We discovered the second group and easily *captured* them as well. We now had seven good men with us, but the captain and the doctor were with John Gold. As a group we could take them, although it would be difficult. Gold's men were loyal, and he would

---

三人是船长的部下，这让我放心了不少。我们向他们扔石头，他们为了不被石头打到，就分散开了。在甘的掩护下，我跑向那些自己人，甘继续朝着金的手下扔石头。

我向船长的部下讲了发生的一切。他们都有手枪，所以我们就包围了金的手下，开枪打他们。他们投降了，乞求不要杀他们。甘帮我们把他们捆了起来，用他们的衬衫袖子堵住了他们的嘴。我们把他们留在了树边。

我们又遇到了第二队人马，同样轻而易举地俘获了他们。现在，我们有七个自己人了。不过，船长和医生还跟金在一起。尽管很难，我们大家一定能把他们救出来。金的手下对他很忠心，为了得到那笔钱，他会不择

---

scatter v. 分散；散开
surrender v. 投降

confront v. 与某人对峙；对抗
capture v. 俘虏

ADVENTURE TRIP I

do anything to get that money.

Chapter Eleven

After nearly an hour, we found them. The doctor and the captain were with John Gold and five of his men. Gunn wanted to separate Gold from the others so that he could get *revenge* for being left behind on the island all those years. He said it was Gold who gave the orders for him to be *marooned*.

We *devised* a plan. I would walk into the open and act like I had been lost all morning. The others would then jump Gold's men and *subdue* them.

I was very nervous. I hate lying, and I was very afraid of Gold. He was a perceptive man, and he might suspect I wasn't telling the truth.

---

revenge *n.* 复仇 maroon *v.* 困住
devise *v.* 修改 subdue *v.* 制服

◆ TREASURE IN THE PUGET SOUND

When I walked into the clearing and greeted the doctor, he seemed relieved to see me. "We thought you were lost, young man," he said.

"I was," I replied. "I'm glad I found you. How is the search going?"

"This cross was nothing. Maybe the others have found something." The doctor had the original map, and he was ready to move to another location.

"Maybe the boy knows more than he reveals," Gold said. His parrot *echoed* him: "The boy knows. The boy knows." The parrot's voice made my spine *crawl*.

"I don't know anything. I was lost all morning," I protested. As I said the words, Gunn and the others raced from the trees and jumped Gold's men. The captain and the doctor quickly realized

---

我走进空地，向医生打招呼，他看见我时，好像松了口气。"我们以为你走丢了呢。"他说。

"我是走丢了。"我回答说，"能找到你们可真开心。找的怎么样了？"

"这个十字标记的地方什么都没有。也许其他人有收获。"医生拿着那张原始的地图，打算去别的地点找。

"也许这个男孩知道点儿什么。"金说。他的鹦鹉也重复着他的话："这个男孩知道。这个男孩知道。"鹦鹉的声音令我毛骨悚然。

"我什么也不知道。我早上就迷路了。"我反驳道。趁着我说话的时候，甘和其他人从树林中冲了出来，扑向金的手下。船长和医生很快反应

---

echo v. 模仿；重复……的话　　　　　　crawl v. （昆虫）爬行

ADVENTURE TRIP I

what was happening and joined the attack. When I took my eye off Gold, he struck me with his crutch. As I got to my feet, he grabbed me by the hair.

One of Gold's men pulled a pistol and started *firing*. He hit three of the captain's men, though the wounds were mild, and they returned fire. I tried to escape, but Gold held me tight. He just stood there like he couldn't be hit. When the firing stopped, only the captain, the doctor, Gold, and I were still standing. All the others had been hit, including Gunn, and some were clearly dead.

"Now let's talk about the money," Gold demanded. "I'll give you young Tim, here, for a *portion* of the money."

"No deal, Gold," the doctor replied.

"Do what he says," I said. "I don't want to die."

过来发生的事，也参加了攻击。一不留神，金就用拐杖打了我一下。我刚要站起来的时候，他一把揪住了我的头发。

金的一个手下掏出手枪，向我们射击。他打中了船长的三名部下，他们都受了轻伤。他们也向金的手下开了枪。我试着逃脱，可金紧紧地抓着我。他就站在那里，丝毫都不怕中弹。枪战结束时，只有船长，医生，金和我还站着。包括甘在内的所有人都中枪了，其中一些人已经死了。

"现在，我们来谈谈那笔钱吧。"金说，"我要用小蒂姆跟你们换一部分钱。"

"别做梦了，金。"医生答道。

"按照他说的做。"我说，"我不想死。"

---

fire *v.* 开火；射击　　　　　　　　　　　　　　portion *n.* 一部分

◆ TREASURE IN THE PUGET SOUND

"Well, then, we have ourselves a *standoff*," Gold said. He seemed to be enjoying the *tension* of the situation. I was *squirming* and he pulled on my hair until I stood still.

I took a deep breath and *summoned up* all the courage I could find. "Gold, I'm the only one who knows where the money is hidden. If you don't let me go, you'll never get any of the money."

"Okay, boy, here's the deal. You lead us to the money, give me a fair share, and I'll let you go. My conditions are that no one tries to kill me, I keep my gun, and I am allowed to leave the island in one of the landing boats. Do we have a deal?"

"Do what he says," I said.

"We have a deal," the captain said. With the agreement, Gold tied a rope around my waist and tied the other end around his waist. He

"看来我们遇到僵局了。"金说。看起来他很享受这种紧张的气氛。我一直在挣扎，他使劲揪住我的头发迫使我站直。

我深深地吸了一口气，鼓足勇气说："金，我是唯一知道藏钱地点的人。如果你不放开我，就永远也得不到那笔钱。"

"好吧。这样吧。你带我们去找钱，给我一部分，我就放了你。我的条件是任何人都不能杀我，我要带着枪，你们给我条小船放我走。怎么样？"

"照他说的做。"我说。

"好吧。"船长说。商定后，金在我的腰上系了根绳子，绳子的另一

standoff *n.* 僵持局面
squirm *v.* 来回扭动

tension *n.* 紧张
summon up 唤起

ADVENTURE TRIP I

kept his gun pointed at my back.

Chapter Twelve

I led them to the *stashed* money, and we began to move the boxes out of the cave, the captain and the doctor doing most of the work. When we were nearly finished, three of Gold's men jumped us. They were wounded, but not badly.

The captain knifed one of them, and Gold shot another. The third man ran when he realized he was now *outnumbered*. When the conflict ended, I was standing against a tree and felt a shooting pain in my left shoulder. I looked down and saw a knife blade sticking out of my shirt and felt warm blood *trickling* down my arm. One of Gold's men had thrown a knife and hit me.

I screamed when the doctor pulled out the blade. It had only

端系在他自己腰上，他用枪顶着我的后背。

第十二章

我把他们带到藏钱的地方，我们开始从洞里往外搬箱子，主要是船长和医生在搬。快搬完的时候，金的三个手下把我们扑倒，他们受了伤，但并无大碍。

船长用刀捅死了一个，金打死了一个。另外那个发现无利可图，就跑掉了。一场混战之后，我靠在一棵树上，感到左肩一阵剧痛。我低下头，看到一把刀露在衬衫外面。我感到一阵热流顺着手臂往下淌，我流血了。金的一个手下向我扔了一把刀，打中了我。

医生拔出刀的时候，我疼得直叫。只是划破了点皮，可疼痛却很强

---

stash *v.* 隐藏　　　　　　　　　　　outnumber *v.* （在数量上）压倒
trickle *v.* 滴；淌

◆ TREASURE IN THE PUGET SOUND

pinched my skin, but the pain was *intense*. I noticed the rope around my waist was loose, and I looked for Gold but didn't see him. Gold was gone. He must have escaped in the *commotion*. Two of the boxes of money were also missing.

After we gathered the *survivors* of the captain's men and helped them to the boat, we loaded the rest of the money onto the ship. We planned to send the police for Gold's men when we arrived back in Seattle.

I think we were all glad to be rid of Gold, and no one seemed too concerned that he had escaped. When we reached Seattle, we turned over the money we had to the authorities. It was much less

---

烈。我注意到腰上的绳子松了，然后开始搜寻金，没有看见他，他跑了。一定是趁乱跑的，同时也少了两箱钱。

我们集合了船长幸存下来的部下，扶他们上了船，把剩下的箱子搬上了船。我们打算回到西雅图后，让警察对付金的那些手下。

能摆脱金，大家都很高兴。大家对于他的逃脱并不十分在意。回到西雅图后，我们把钱交给了国家。我们找到的只是一少部分。我们猜想一定

---

pinch *v.* 夹紧；捏住
commotion *n.* 骚动；骚乱

intense *adj.* 强烈的
survivor *n.* 幸存者

ADVENTURE TRIP I

than the total missing. We figured there was still some money that Gunn had stashed on the island. We were given a reward of $25,000, a lot less than the money we could have kept, but it was enough. There was plenty of money in my share to help my parents fix their inn.

So, that is the story of the treasure in Puget Sound. It is an *unpleasant* memory I have recorded, but it needed to be told. To this day, I still have *nightmares*. I still can hear Gold's parrot: "The boy knows. The boy knows."

是甘还在其他的地方藏了钱。政府给了我们两万五千美元作为奖励。虽然比起我们找到的钱，这些奖励微不足道，但这些已经足够维修我爸妈的旅馆了。

这就是普吉湾宝藏的故事。虽然我讲述的不是愉快的经历，但是大家需要了解真相。直到今天，我还会做噩梦。仍然能听到金的鹦鹉的声音："这个男孩知道。这个男孩知道。"

---

unpleasant　*adj.*　不愉快的　　　　　　　　　nightmare　*n.*　噩梦

♦ IN HUCK'S SHOES

04

In Huck's Shoes

Anything for Adventure

Clear the tables, *chop* the onions, bake the bread—Miguel Ventura was tired of all the work he had to do in his family's sandwich shop.

"It's not fair. I'm only eleven," he said to his Mom. "Saturdays are supposed to be fun."

成为哈克

只想冒险

收拾桌子，切洋葱，烤面包——米格尔·文图拉讨厌在家里的三明治店里不得不做的所有工作。

"这不公平，我只有十一岁。"他对妈妈说，"星期六应该充满乐趣。"

chop *v.* 切碎

ADVENTURE TRIP 1

"Sorry, Miguel," she said, "but you're the oldest. Teresa's only seven." His little sister *zipped* across the shop *bouncing* a ball.

His dad unlocked the front door, saying, "She's right, we need you to help out."

The pit of Miguel's stomach ached—and not from hunger. Adventure and freedom seemed a million miles away. "Unless…" he whispered, looking toward the shop's backroom.

A few months ago, Miguel climbed an old, red ladder that led up to a loft in the backroom. He discovered a chest full of *enchanted* books that belonged to his great-grandpa George, a magician called The Great Gallardo.

"我很抱歉，米格尔。"她说，"可是，你是家里最大的孩子，特丽莎只有七岁。"他的妹妹在店里跑来跑去地拍着球。

他的父亲边打开前门边说："你妈妈说得对，我们需要你来帮忙。"

米格尔感到胃里一阵刺痛——不是因为饥饿，而是因为冒险和自由好像离他十万八千里了。"除非……"他嘀咕着，向商店后屋看去。

几个月前，米格尔爬上了一个破旧的红梯子，一直爬到了后屋的阁楼。他发现了一个满是魔法书的箱子，箱子的主人是他的曾祖父乔治。他是一个被称为"伟大的盖拉多"的魔法师。

---

zip *v.* 快速移动
enchanted *adj.* 着了魔的

bounce *v.* （使）弹起；（使）反弹

◆ IN HUCK'S SHOES

Somehow, after reading a passage from one of the magical books, Miguel was *transported* into the story as one of the characters. Through the Great Gallardo's books, Miguel had met Benjamin Franklin, battled a *terrifying* space monster, and become a cowboy in the Old West!

Miguel raced to the backroom and climbed the ladder, skipping the broken *rung*. He had just enough time before the lunch rush to discover his next adventure.

Being Huckleberry

The old *skeleton key* stuck out of the lock in the magical, black chest, and Miguel turned it with a click. He grabbed the first book,

---

不知怎么地，米格尔翻看一本书，读了一页后，就被带入了书中的世界，成了故事中的人物。通过伟大的盖拉多的书，米格尔遇见了本杰明·富兰克林，与恐怖的太空怪物搏斗，还成了一个西部的牛仔！

米格尔跑到后屋，爬上梯子，跳过了那个断裂的梯级。午饭高峰期到来之前，他刚好有足够的时间，进行下一次探险。

成为哈克贝利

米格尔把那把古老的万能钥匙插入了那只神奇的黑箱子，转了一下钥匙，听到了咔嗒一声响。他抓起第一本书——《汤姆·索亚历险记》，他

---

transport *v.* 使身处他境
rung *n.* 梯级

terrifying *adj.* 可怕的
skeleton key 万能钥匙

ADVENTURE TRIP I

The Adventures of Tom Sawyer, and he couldn't wait to see which of Tom's classic adventures he'd be pulled into. A feather marked page 91, and a sentence jumped out at him like it was in three *dimensions*. Miguel read aloud. "They shoved off presently, Tom in command, Huck at the after and Joe at the forward."

The words of the next sentence danced around on the page... *folded arms, Tom amid ships, and gave with stood and gloomy-browed orders low, his a stern whisper in.*

Miguel closed his eyes to fight off the *dizziness* as cool air whispered across his face.

"Bring her to the wind!" a voice shouted.

迫不及待地想看看他会被带入汤姆的哪个经典历险中。一片羽毛夹在91页上，上面的一句话跳到了他眼前，看起来好像是立体的。米格尔大声地读出来："他们立刻上船出发了，汤姆指挥，哈克在船尾，乔在船头。"

下个句子的字在书页上跳动起来……"汤姆站在船中间，张开双臂，……"

米格尔闭上眼睛，想赶走眩晕，这时，一阵清凉的风吹过了他的脸庞。

"向着风的方向划！"一个声音喊道。

---

dimension n. 维（构成空间的因素）　　　　dizziness n. 眩晕

◆ IN HUCK'S SHOES

Miguel opened his eyes to find himself sailing down a river, rowing at the left *oar*!

"I'm Huck Finn!" he yelled, looking down at his bare feet and *scraggly* pants.

"That ye be!" the boy at the *bow* called. "Now bring her 'round!"

"Aye, aye, sir!" Miguel smiled ear-to-ear, breathing in adventure with every breath.

Tom Sawyer was short and wore a black *bandanna* on his head. The tall, skinny kid at the stern was Tom's friend, Joe Harper. In the story, Miguel remembered that the three boys ran away to become pirates on Jackson's Island.

米格尔睁开眼睛，发现自己正在河上航行，摇着船左边的桨。

"我是哈克·费恩！"他低头看到了自己赤裸的双脚和破烂的裤子，大叫道。

"你当然是！"在船头的那个人说。"现在朝相反的方向划！"

"是，是，长官！"米格尔咧开嘴笑了，他闻到了探险的味道。

汤姆·索亚个子不高，头上围了一块黑色的大手绢。高高瘦瘦的在船尾的是汤姆的朋友乔·哈勃。米格尔记得在故事中，这三个男孩从家里跑了出来，去杰克逊岛上做海盗。

---

oar *n.* 桨
bow *n.* 船头

scraggly *adj.* 散乱的
bandanna *n.* 头巾

ADVENTURE TRIP I

◆ IN HUCK'S SHOES

The boys rowed quietly past a distant town lit by a few *glimmering* lights.

Finally, Tom called out, "I am the Black *Avenger* of the Spanish Main!"

"I am the Terror of the Seas!" yelled Joe.

Both boys looked at Miguel, who *swallowed* hard.

"And Finn, the Red-Handed, what do ye say for yerself?" Tom asked.

"I... I... say THERE GOES JACKSON'S ISLAND!" Miguel called as the current *swiftly* swept them by it.

Tom scrambled about the raft, shouting orders, "Act lively now, mates!"

男孩们静静地划过了远处的一个村子，村子里只有几点微弱的灯光。
后来，汤姆大喊道："我是西班牙海上的黑衣复仇天使！"
"我是海上魔王！"乔大叫。
他们俩都看着米格尔，米格尔哑口无言。
"费恩，手上沾满血的费恩，你说什么？"汤姆问。
"我……我……说我们到杰克逊岛了！"米格尔喊。这时，他们来到了一处水流湍急处。
汤姆在木筏上摇晃了一下，发号着施令："加把劲呀，伙计们！"

---

glimmering　*n.*　微光
swallow　*v.*　（由于紧张）做吞咽动作

avenger　*n.*　复仇者
swiftly　*adv.*　迅速地

ADVENTURE TRIP I

Miguel rowed hard along the tree-covered island until his arms ached, and the raft finally grounded itself on a *sandbar*.

Tom and Joe created a roaring fire. "For the feast!" Joe said. Both boys revealed two *succulent* hams that they had 'borrowed' for the trip.

"What's in yer bag, Huck?" Tom asked.

Miguel suddenly became aware of the weight on his back.

"A *skillet*!" said Joe as he opened Miguel's bag. "To fry the bacon!" Joe continued as he tossed in slices of ham. As they *sizzled* over the flames, Miguel's stomach grumbled.

"We will be the grandest sort of pirates." Tom said, pacing and marching around the fire. "Doing as we please. Maybe we'll bury

---

米格尔沿着郁郁葱葱的小岛使劲地划，一直划得胳膊都疼了，木筏才终于搁浅在了一个沙堤上。

汤姆和乔升了一堆火。"开饭吧！"乔说。他们俩拿出了两个美味多汁的火腿，这是他们为这次旅行特意"借"来的。

"你的袋子里有什么，哈克？"汤姆问。

米格尔突然意识到了背后的重量。

"平底锅！"乔打开米格尔的袋子说，"用来煎培根！"乔扔过来几片火腿继续说。火腿在火上烤着，发出嘶嘶的响声，米格尔的肚子饿得咕咕直叫。

"我们会成为最伟大的海盗。"汤姆围着火来回地踱着步说，"我们

---

sandbar *n.* 沙洲
skillet *n.* 平底煎锅

succulent *adj.* 多汁的
sizzle *v.* 发出咝咝声

◆ IN HUCK'S SHOES

some treasure tonight, so the ghosts will watch over it."

The wind *howled*. Tom howled back.

"No responsibilities!" said Joe.

"No waking up in the morning, doing chores, going to school or to church," Tom said. "More of a carefree life for you, Hucky?"

"I am Finn, the Red-Handed, and it's a pirate's life for me!" Miguel's duties back at his family's shop *vanished* as he curled up next to the campfire. He let go of his *wakefulness*, and let in the freedom of his new life as a pirate.

在做我们喜欢的事。也许我们今天晚上会去埋些珠宝，这样，才会有魔鬼来看守。"

狂风怒吼，汤姆也对着风大吼。

"不用负责任！"乔说。

"不用早起，做家务，去学校或是教堂。"汤姆说，"对你来说，是更加自由自在的生活，哈克，你说呢？"

"我是费恩，手上沾满了血，海盗的生活正适合我！"米格尔留在家里的店里的责任都消失了，他蜷着身子，坐在篝火旁。米格尔把现实抛到了脑后，沉浸在做海盗的自由自在的新生活中。

---

howl *v.* 咆哮　　　　　　　　　　　　vanish *v.* 消失
wakefulness *n.* 不眠

ADVENTURE TRIP I

Skeeter Fever

The *eerie* silence of the woods woke Miguel in the morning. Joe was sprawled against the log next to him, but Tom was nowhere to be seen.

Miguel thought of his family, and a slight pain *clenched* his heart. He'd never been gone this long before in one of the Great Gallardo's books, and although he was enjoying his newfound freedom, he hoped that time passed differently when he was away. He didn't want his parents to worry.

"Huck!" Tom ran up to him. "Look what I discovered on the raft!"

Miguel did not move as Tom held up a leather *sack*, the size of a marble bag.

蚊子高烧

早上，米格尔在森林中诡异的寂静中醒来。乔躺在他身边的圆木上，可是，汤姆不知道去哪儿了。

米格尔想到了他的家人，心里有些不安，他从来没在盖拉多的书中待过这么久。尽管他正享受着刚刚得到的自由，他还是希望他不在时，家里的时间过得慢些。他不想让父母担心。

"哈克！"汤姆向他跑过来。"看我在木筏里找到了什么！"

汤姆拿着一个皮包，跟大理石条纹口袋一样大小。米格尔坐在那里没动。

---

eerie *adj.* 怪异的
sack *n.* 麻袋

clench *v.* 捏紧；攥紧

◆ IN HUCK'S SHOES

With trembling hands, Miguel tugged open the bag and *gasped*. Twenty gold coins! Miguel asked, "Do you know who they belong to?"

"This raft must have belonged to some real pirates," Tom guessed with awe.

Uh-oh. Miguel did not remember this storyline from the book.

"Real pirates?" Joe questioned, half-asleep.

Tom nodded. "They pirates probably have been looking for their raft," Tom said. "It's only a matter of time till they find it."

Miguel's heart sank.

"We're gonna give everything back, right?" Joe asked, now awake.

"*Heck*, no!" Tom said. "We are pirates, too. We'll bury the gold at

---

米格尔用颤抖的手用力拉开了包，里面有二十个金币！米格尔问："你知道是谁的吗？"

"木筏一定属于真正的海盗。"汤姆敬畏地猜道。

哦，噢。米格尔不记得书上的这一段。

"真正的海盗？"乔迷迷糊糊地问。

汤姆点点头。"他们这些海盗也许一直在寻找木筏。"汤姆说，"找到它只是时间问题。"

米格尔心里一沉。

"我们会把东西都送回去，对吧？"乔现在完全醒了，问。

"见鬼，当然不会！"汤姆说，"我们也是海盗。我们要在今晚午夜

---

gasp v. （尤指由于惊讶等）倒抽气　　　heck n. 真见鬼（hell委婉的说法）

ADVENTURE TRIP 1

midnight tonight."

Gulp.

"Pirates have swords, knives, and guns," Joe *muttered*. "All we have is a pocketknife and a *bunch* of fishhooks."

"Yeah, but we got these." Tom pointed to his brain. "We're smarter than any pirate I've ever met."

After searching the island, they found a damp cave in which to hide their supplies. "All we need to do," Tom said, "is to fill up the coin bag with rocks and put it back on the raft. Then, we'll take the raft a mile downriver."

"To make it look like the current swept it away," Joe said.

"They won't *suspect* it had been pirated," Tom said.

把金子埋起来。"

一片哑然。

"海盗手里有剑，有刀，还有枪。"乔嘟囔着，"我们只有一把折叠小刀和几只鱼钩。"

"是的，不过我们有这个。"汤姆指着他的脑袋说，"我们比我遇到过的所有海盗都聪明。"

他们在岛上找了一圈后，找到了一个潮湿的山洞，把他们的东西藏在了里面。"我们需要做的是，"汤姆说，"用石头把装金币的袋子装满，把它放回到木筏上。然后，我们把木筏带到下游一英里的地方。"

"使它看起来像是水流把它冲走了的样子。"乔说。

"他们不会想到有人打劫了木筏。"汤姆说。

mutter *v.* 嘀咕；嘟囔　　　　　　　　　　　　bunch *n.* 串
suspect *v.* 怀疑

◆ IN HUCK'S SHOES

Something wasn't right. No gold or pirates existed on Jackson's Island in The Adventures of Tom Sawyer. This just didn't make sense.

On their way back after grounding the raft farther down the river, a gunshot shattered the still air. "The pirates!" Tom whispered. "We've got to bury the *booty*!"

Using pieces of *splintered* shale, Tom, Huck, and Joe dug *furiously* in front of an ancient, oak tree. Tom dumped the coins into his marble bag. He *chucked* it in the hole and filled it up.

A branch broke behind them. Miguel held up the lantern to find three of the ugliest pirates they'd ever seen! The first one was tiny, the second a few feet taller, and the third pirate stood as tall as a professional basketball player. All three of them were covered in red, pus-oozing mosquito bites!

有点不对劲！在汤姆·索亚历险记中杰克逊岛上没有出现金币或者海盗。这件事不对劲。

他们把木筏扔在了河下游更远的地方。在回来的路上，一声枪响打破了平静。"是那些海盗！"汤姆小声说，"我们得把金币藏起来！"

汤姆，哈克和乔用岩石碎片在一棵古老的橡树前面拼命地挖了一个坑出来。汤姆把金币倒入他的花纹口袋，放在洞里，埋上了土。

他们身后的一个树枝断裂了，米格尔提起灯笼，看见了三个他们见到过的最丑陋的海盗。第一个身材矮小，第二个比第一个高点，第三个跟职业篮球队员一样高。他们三个浑身上下都是红色的，蚊子叮的包！

---

booty *n.* 赃物
furiously *adv.* 猛烈地

splinter *v.* 裂成碎片
chuck *v.* 扔；抛

ADVENTURE TRIP 1

"What're ye laddies think yer up to?" The tall one *scratched* his neck and held out his sword.

Joe looked at Miguel, who looked at Tom.

"Just burying our cat," Tom said.

"Yer cat?" the medium one asked as he *slapped* his forehead.

"He died of the fever," Tom said.

"The fever?" questioned the short one, picking at a *nasty* bite on his chin.

"Mosquito fever," Joe *chimed in*, causing the three pirates to gulp.

"The rain's been fierce this year," Tom said.

"All them skeeters brought a nasty disease with them," Joe said.

"你们这些小子干什么呢？"最高的那个一边挠着他的脖子，一边拔出剑。
乔看了看米格尔，米格尔看了看汤姆。
"只是在埋我们的猫。"汤姆说。
"你的猫？"中等身材的那个拍了一下额头问。
"它死于高烧。"汤姆说。
"高烧？"矮个子的那个用手抠着下巴上的大包问。
"蚊子高烧。"乔补充了一句，那三个海盗都不出声了。
"今年的雨特别多。"汤姆说。
"它们这些蚊子带来了一种可怕的疾病。"乔说。

---

scratch *v.* 挠；搔　　　　　　　　　　　slap *v.* 拍
nasty *adj.* 令人厌恶的　　　　　　　　　chime in 插嘴

♦ IN HUCK'S SHOES

"What kind of disease?" asked the medium pirate. "Because we fell asleep last night, and those *blasted* bugs ate us alive!"

"It eats away your flesh first," Miguel said, without thinking, "then your organs." Maybe he was becoming a pirate, after all.

Tom and Joe almost laughed.

The pirates stood there, scratching every inch of *exposed* skin.

"But don't worry," Tom said. "You can stop the fever."

"How?" they shouted.

"By not scratching," Joe added.

The pirates *froze*. Then, the short pirate slapped his leg, the medium one rubbed his neck, and the tall guy scraped his arms

---

"什么样的疾病？"中等个头儿的那个海盗问，"因为我们昨天晚上睡着了，那些该死的蚊子把我们咬得够呛！"
"这种病会先腐蚀掉你的肉。"米格尔想也没想地说，"然后是你的器官。"也许他已经开始成为海盗了。
汤姆和乔差点没笑出声来。
那些海盗站在那，抓挠着露在外面的每一寸肌肤。
"但是，不用担心。"汤姆说，"你可以阻止高烧。"
"怎么阻止？"他们喊道。
"只要不抓就可以。"乔接着说。
海盗们僵住了。然后，那个矮个子海盗拍打着大腿，中等个儿的那个

---

blasted *adj.* 该死的；可恶的   exposed *adj.* 无遮蔽的
freeze *v.* 僵住；呆住

ADVENTURE TRIP I

against the *bark* of a tree. "We can't stop scraaaatchiiing!"

"I do know a way," said Tom, as he *winked* at Miguel and Joe. "Follow me."

They headed back to the sandbar where the pirates' raft was grounded on the beach again. "This yours?" Tom asked.

"Yep," the tall one said, as he danced around to stop from scratching. "We just found it after it *drifted* away from us a day ago."

Miguel eyed the small sack of marbles through the *slats* of the crate on the raft.

"Tell us how to stop the itch, boy." The short pirate clenched his

抓挠着脖子，高的那个在树皮上蹭着胳膊。"我们忍不住抓痒！"

"我知道一个办法。"汤姆说着向米格尔和乔眨了眨眼睛。"跟我来。"

他们走到了沙堤，海盗的船又停在了那里，"这是你们的吗？"汤姆问。

"是的。"那个高个子的说着转起了圈，极力克制着抓痒。"我们刚刚找回它，一天前，它被水冲走了。"

米格尔透过木筏上木板箱的板条看到了那个装着石头的袋子。

"告诉我们怎么才能止痒，小孩。"那个矮个子的海盗咬着牙，用一

bark n. 树皮   wink v. 眨眼
drift v. 漂流   slat n. 板条

◆ IN HUCK'S SHOES

teeth, and pointed a sharp knife at them.

"This is what you do," Tom said, taking the pirates down the beach.

Soon thereafter, the boys saw the pirates sailing away on the raft—their bodies coated in white sand!

"Now don't move," Tom shouted, "until the sun *hardens* that sand!" He laughed. "This is the only way to rid yerselves of the *itch*!"

They waited, in silence, until the pirates were out of sight.

"*Shiver* me timbers!" Joe shouted. "You did it, Tom!"

"The pirate king!" Miguel bowed down. "This is the greatest day of my life!"

"I couldn't have done it without me mates. Arrgh," he said, as

---

把锋利的刀指着他们问。

"你们得这么做。"汤姆说着带着海盗们下了海。

很快，孩子们就看到海盗们站在木筏上漂走了——他们的身上涂了一层白沙。

"现在，不要动，"汤姆喊，"直到太阳把沙子晒干！"他大声笑着，"这是唯一能止痒的办法。"

他们默默地等着，直到海盗们消失在视线中。

"吓死我了！"乔喊道，"你做到了，汤姆！"

"海盗王！"米格尔弯下腰。"这是我一生中最棒的一天！"

"没有你们的帮忙，我做不到。"他说。他们穿过树林，挖出金币，

---

harden v. （使）变硬　　　　　　　　　　　　itch n. 痒
shiver v. （因恐惧）颤抖

ADVENTURE TRIP I

they rushed through the trees to unbury their booty, dancing and singing their favorite pirate *tune*.

Back on Track

That night, the boys slept hard, dreaming of their *devious* pirate tricks. When they awoke, a strange *swishing* sound came from the river.

"What's that?" Miguel asked.

"Sounds like..." Joe started.

"...the steamboat!" Tom finished.

Joe and Tom always finished each other's sentences because that's what good friends did. Miguel began to miss his own best friends.

他们唱着最喜欢的海盗歌，并随着歌声翩翩起舞。

回到正轨

那天晚上，孩子们睡得很香，梦到了他们狡猾的海盗把戏。他们醒来时，听到河边传来一阵奇怪的嗖嗖的响声。

"那是什么？"米格尔问。

"听起来像……"乔开口说。

"……轮船！"汤姆接着说。

乔和汤姆总是能接上彼此的话，因为好朋友的默契。米格尔开始想念自己的好朋友了。

---

tune *n.* 曲调；曲子　　　　　　　　devious *adj.* 狡猾的；不坦诚的
swish *v.* 发嗖；嗖声

◆ IN HUCK'S SHOES

Boom! A *cannonball* shot rang out from the steamboat.

"Someone has drowned!" Joe said as they listened carefully to people calling out from the decks of the steamboat.

"Not just anyone," Tom said, smiling. "They think we've drowned!"

Miguel remembered this part of the story well. Tom was just about to make the trip home to leave a note for Aunt Polly to tell her he was safe.

"We're heroes!" Joe said.

"We're the talk of the town!" Tom said.

That night, around the fire, Joe became homesick. "I just can't let my ma suffer so."

"Terror of the Seas!" Tom shouted. "There's no stoppin' us, now."

嘭！从轮船上发射出了一枚炮弹。

"有人淹死了！"乔说，他们仔细地听着轮船甲板上人们的呼叫声。

"不只是那个人。"汤姆笑着说，"他们以为我们都淹死了！"

米格尔清清楚楚地记得故事的这部分。汤姆正要回家，给波莉阿姨留个纸条，告诉她，他很安全。

"我们是英雄！"乔说。

"我们是镇子里的话题！"汤姆说。

那天晚上，大家围在火边。乔开始想家。"我只是不想让我妈太担心。"

"海上魔王！"汤姆高声喊，"我们现在不能停下来。"他吹着口

---

cannonball *n.* 炮弹

ADVENTURE TRIP I

He whistled, *entranced* by the gold coins.

Joe looked at Miguel, who *shrugged*.

"Don't ya think, Hucky?" Tom said. "You've lived the carefree life. Tell Joe he doesn't need to go back."

Miguel had mixed emotions. He was having the time of his life, and yet part of him felt like Joe. He knew his parents would miss him terribly, and he missed them too, even his sister, Teresa.

Miguel *hesitated*.

"Huckleberry Finn, here, thinks you ought to continue your newfound life as a pirate. Your family will go on without you," Tom answered.

Those words sent a shiver down Miguel's *spine*. Tom seemed to

---

哨，痴迷地看着金币。

乔看了看米格尔，米格尔耸了耸肩。

"你不这样认为吗，哈克？"汤姆说，"你过着自由自在的生活，告诉乔他不需要回去。"

米格尔的表情很复杂。他过着自己向往的生活，然而，他也跟乔有一样的感受。他知道父母会很想念他，他也想他们，甚至也想妹妹特丽莎。

米格尔犹豫了。

"哈克贝利·费恩，我想你应该继续过海盗的新生活。你的家人没你也会继续活下去。"汤姆回答。

这些话说得米格尔脊背发凉。汤姆看起来已经完全忘了爱他的那些

---

entrance *v.* 使狂喜；使入迷
hesitate *v.* 犹豫

shrug *v.* 耸肩
spine *n.* 脊柱

◆ IN HUCK'S SHOES

have forgotten about all of the people who loved him. With his *scruffy* clothes and *matted* hair, Tom Sawyer looked like he was turning into a full-fledged pirate!

Miguel worried that *The Adventures of Tom Sawyer* wasn't unfolding as it should. He had to *remedy* that, and quickly.

That night, after Joe fell asleep, Tom and Miguel huddled around the fire.

"I'm surprised you didn't help me *convince* Joe," Tom said. "You love freedom more than anyone I know, Huck."

"I… I think that…" Miguel said. "You don't appreciate what you have."

"What?" Tom's mouth gaped.

人。穿着破破烂烂的衣服，顶着一头乱蓬蓬的头发，汤姆·索亚看起来已经变成了一个十足的海盗！

米格尔感到很担心《汤姆·索亚历险记》没有按照故事中的情节发展。他必须迅速地把它纠正过来。

那天晚上，乔睡着后，汤姆和米格尔围坐在篝火旁。

"你没有帮我说服乔，我感到很奇怪。"汤姆说，"你比我认识的所有人都喜欢自由，哈克。"

"我……我想……"米格尔说，"你对自己拥有的并不感激。"

"什么？"汤姆张大了嘴巴。

---

scruffy *adj.* 不整洁的；邋遢的
remedy *v.* 改进；纠正

matted *adj.* 乱蓬蓬的
convince *v.* 说服；劝说

ADVENTURE TRIP I

"Your Aunt Polly loves you," Miguel said. "Sure, you've got to get up and do chores and go to school, but she relies on you, Tom," Miguel said. "She wants you to be a better person."

"You sound like her right now." Tom turned away in *disgust*. "You *betray* the life of the pirate, Huck."

An *owl* hooted from the tree above. Miguel stood up and tossed a stone into the river. "It may not feel like it now, but things will get better, and you'll see how much your aunt's love means." Miguel sounded like his own mother, but he'd do anything to save The Adventures of Tom Sawyer.

"Arrgh!" Tom *spit* into the fire. "I'm a good pirate, I am! And now

---

"你的波莉阿姨爱你。"米格尔说，"是的，你得起床、做家务、去上学。不过，她不能没有你，汤姆。"米格尔说："她想让你做好人。"

"你现在听起来很像她。"汤姆厌恶地扭过头去。"你背叛了海盗的生活，哈克。"

一只猫头鹰在头上的树上叫着。米格尔站起来，向河里扔了一块石头。"也许现在看起来是这样，不过，事情会越来越好，你就会知道你阿姨的爱对你有多么重要。"米格尔听起来像自己的妈妈，但是，为了挽救《汤姆·索亚历险记》，他愿意做任何事。

汤姆向火中吐了一口唾沫说："我是一个好海盗，我就是！既然每个

---

disgust *n.* 厌恶　　　　　　　　　　　betray *v.* 背叛
owl *n.* 猫头鹰　　　　　　　　　　　spit *v.* 吐唾沫

◆ IN HUCK'S SHOES

that everyone thinks I'm dead, I can start over fresh."

"Things will work out if you let them know you're safe," Miguel said. "You'll have many adventures—believe me."

Tom looked up at the stars.

"And grownups can help you out in *scary* times," Miguel whispered. "Don't be afraid to ask when you need it."

"You've gone soft, Huck." Tom pulled his bandanna low over his eyes to sleep.

Miguel curled up too, wondering if Tom would slip out that night to visit his family, like in the story.

A *coyote* howled, and Miguel opened his eyes in the darkness just

---

人都认为我死了，我就可以重新开始做海盗了。"

"如果你让他们知道你很安全，就没事了。"米格尔说，"你会有很多冒险经历，相信我。"

汤姆抬头看看天上的星星。

"大人们会帮你摆脱这种提心吊胆的日子。"米格尔低声说，"当你需要的时候，不要害怕求助。"

"你太软弱了，哈克。"汤姆把头巾拉下来遮住眼睛，睡觉了。

米格尔也蜷起身子，想知道汤姆会不会像故事中那样，在晚上溜出去回家。

听到了一声狼叫，米格尔在黑暗中睁开眼睛，还没到黎明。乔在他旁

---

scary *adj.* 害怕的   coyote *n.* 丛林狼；草原狼

ADVENTURE TRIP I

before dawn. Joe *snored* next to him, but Tom had vanished in the night. Miguel found a rolled piece of bark that read:

Huck,

Thanks for the truthful words, wherever you got them. Life in the woods has made you wise, Finn the Red-Handed! Be back in a few days. Take care of Joe!

Tom

Miguel smiled. Now everything was back on track!

The trees began to *blur* so he closed his eyes. The warmth of the campfire faded, and Miguel realized that he was back in the loft. The smell of freshly baked bread made his heart flutter. Being a pirate

---

边打着呼噜。但是，汤姆在夜里不见了。米格尔发现了一块卷着的树皮，上面写着：

哈克，

　　感谢你的肺腑之言，不管你是从哪儿学来的。树林中的生活使你变得聪明了。费恩，沾满鲜血的费恩！我过几天就会回去，照顾好乔！

汤姆

米格尔笑了。现在一切都回到了正轨！

树木开始变得模糊起来，于是，他闭上了眼睛。温暖的篝火一点点地消失了，米格尔意识到自己回到了阁楼。新出炉的面包的味道使他很激

---

snore *v.* 打呼噜　　　　　　　　　　truthful *adj.* 真实的；诚实的
blur *v.* （使）变得模糊不清

◆ IN HUCK'S SHOES

was exciting, but Miguel was happy to be home.

"Miguel!" his Dad called. "Lunch rush is here! I need you to make a few bacon *deluxe* sandwiches for me."

Miguel looked at his watch—realizing only minutes had passed since he'd come up to the loft. "Aye, aye, sir!" he answered. "I'll do anything for a little adventure!"

动。做海盗很令人激动,但是,回到家里,米格尔感到很高兴。

"米格尔!"他爸爸喊,"午饭高峰期到了!我需要你帮我做几个培根豪华三明治。"

米格尔看看手表——意识到从他上阁楼到现在,才过去了几分钟。"是的,是的,长官!"他答道,"为了冒险,我愿意做任何事情!"

---

deluxe *adj.* 豪华的

ADVENTURE TRIP I

05

In the Name of Discovery

An Explorer's Life

A Spanish *fleet* sailed across the page in Miguel's social studies book.

"Gold, power, *glory*," Miguel's friend, Trevon, exclaimed, "those explorers really had it all!"

"Sailing to unknown lands, seeing new things, adventure around every corner... boys!" Lily exclaimed.

以发现之名

探险家的生活

米格尔的社会研究书上印着一支航行中的西班牙舰队。

"金钱，权力，荣誉。"米格尔的朋友特莱文高声说，"那些探险者真是什么都得到了！"

"坐船去探索未知的土地，目睹新鲜的事物，险象环生……男孩们！"莉莉说。

---

fleet *n.* 舰队   glory *n.* 荣誉

◆ IN THE NAME OF DISCOVERY

"Yeah, we love an adventure!" said Trevon.

Miguel couldn't argue with the idea that exploring the world five hundred years ago could have been exciting. That's what he'd realized after studying some of the famous explorers such as Sir Francis Drake, "The Dragon," a feared *privateer*, *navigator*, and seaman. Drake was one of the first Englishmen to sail all the way around the world, and was best known for *plundering* the Spanish *colonies* in the New World in search of treasure.

"I wonder what it was like?" Miguel asked.

"What do you mean?" Trevon said. "It must have been totally awesome!"

"What do you mean? It had to have been scary!" Lily added.

Miguel imagined himself at the helm of a huge ship, leading an

---

"是呀，我们都喜欢冒险！"特莱文说。

米格尔对这点丝毫不怀疑。在五百年前，探索世界一定很令人激动。在学习了一些著名的探险家的故事后，他意识到这点。比如，"大龙"弗朗西斯·德雷克爵士，一位令人敬畏的私掠者、航海家、海员。德雷克是第一位乘船环游世界的英国人，他因为在美洲大陆上打劫西班牙殖民者、掠夺财物而闻名于世。

"我真想看看那时候的探险是什么样子的？"米格尔问。

"你是什么意思？"特莱文说，"当然是超级棒！"

"你们真这么想吗？那时候一定很可怕！"莉莉补充道。

米格尔想象着自己指挥着一艘巨轮，在一望无际的大海上，引领着

---

privateer *n.* 私掠者
plunder *v.* 掠夺
navigator *n.* 航海家
colony *n.* 殖民地

ADVENTURE TRIP I

armada across the open sea. Gold coins would *burst* from his pockets while men surrounded him, acting upon his every command. In his mind, Miguel stood taller than ever. It made his real life feel as boring as watching paint dry.

"Yeah, it must have been totally exciting," Miguel said *dreamily* as he stood up and walked to the window. "But you do know that most of what they did was totally dishonest and cruel, right? A lot of *innocent* people were killed. Entire villages were destroyed just so these explorers could go home wealthy."

"That was hundreds of years ago," Trevon said.

"It was still wrong," Lily said.

"Just imagine how greed and glory made these guys do crazy

一支无敌舰队。他的口袋里装满了金币，人们围着他转，对他唯命是从。在他的心里，米格尔好像高大了许多。这使他的现实生活显得那么索然无味。

"是的，那一定很带劲。"米格尔站起来，走到窗前，入神地想象着。"不过，你也知道他们的大多数行为都是不道德的、凶残的，对吧？许多无辜的人失去了生命。整个村庄被洗劫一空，只是为了满足这些探险者的一己私欲。"

"那是几百年前的事了。"特莱文说。

"即使在那个时候，这也是不对的。"莉莉说。

"想象一下，什么样的贪婪和荣誉会使这些人做出这么疯狂的举动。"

---

armada *n.* 无敌舰队
dreamily *adv.* 似在梦中地

burst *v.* 充满，塞满
innocent *adj.* 无辜的

◆ IN THE NAME OF DISCOVERY

things, things they probably wouldn't do under normal *circumstances*, all in the name of discovery," replied Miguel.

On the walk home, Miguel wondered what he might be willing to give up in the name of adventure and discovery. Would he hurt or steal? He thought no, but he wasn't sure what risks he would take. How far would he go to find the *ultimate* discovery?

That evening, after doing his homework, Miguel wandered up the old red ladder to his favorite place—the loft. Thoughts of gold-searching explorers *drifted* through his mind. He reached out to open the Great Gallardo's chest when something slipped and clanked to the ground. It was a rusty, metal dagger with a jagged, worn blade. Miguel wondered what other secrets the mysterious and *enchanted* trunk held.

这些事在正常的情况下,他们也许根本不会做。这一切都打着发现的名义。"米格尔回应道。

在回家的路上,米格尔在想,在探索和发现的名义下,他可能心甘情愿的放弃什么东西。他会去伤人或者偷盗吗?他想自己不会那么做。但是,他不确定,自己会不会铤而走险。为了最终的发现,他会走出多远呢?

那天晚上,做完作业后,米格尔爬上那个破旧的红色梯子,来到了他最喜欢的地方——阁楼。淘金者的形象在他的脑海中,挥之不去。他走过去,打开伟大的盖拉多的箱子。这时候,一个东西掉了下来,砸在了地上。是一把锈迹斑斑的金属匕首。匕首的刀刃已经磨损成了锯齿状。米格尔很想知道,这只神奇的魔法箱里,还承载着怎样的秘密。

---

circumstance *n.* 环境,境遇
drift *v.* 浮现;漂浮

ultimate *adj.* 最后的
enchant *v.* 使入迷,使迷惑

ADVENTURE TRIP I

Miguel pulled from the chest a black leather-bound book titled *Journey to the Center of the Earth* by Jules Verne. Miguel's dad had read the story to him last year when he had been sick at home with the *mumps*. "I remember this dagger," he said, "or at least one just like it. It belonged to an explorer from Iceland, Arne Saknussemm. According to the book, Arne was the first man to travel to the center of Earth." Then Miguel also remembered his favorite character, Hans. He admired Hans's *adventurous* spirit and bravery.

Miguel's heart *pounded*. He knew if he opened the book, he would be taking a journey, and there was no telling what might be in store for him. Miguel opened the book and started to read… *"My uncle ventured beneath the gigantic groves. I followed him, though not without a certain apprehension …"*

米格尔从箱子里取出一本黑色皮面书。书名为《地心历险记》，是朱丽斯·凡尔纳的作品。去年他得腮腺炎在家休养时，米格尔的爸爸给他读过这本书。"我记得这把匕首。"他说，"或者跟它类似的匕首。它属于一个冰岛的探险家安·沙克纳塞姆。根据这本书的记载，安是第一个到地心探险的人。"接着，米格尔也想起了书中他最喜欢的人物汉斯。他敬佩汉斯的冒险精神和英勇气概。

米格尔的心怦怦直跳。他知道，如果翻开书，他就会经历一场冒险之旅。没有人知道会有什么样的危险等着他。米格尔翻开书，开始看……"叔叔在巨大的树丛中探险，我跟在他身后，尽管不知道……"

---

mumps *n.* 腮腺炎	adventurous *adj.* 爱冒险的
pound *v.* （心脏）狂跳	apprehension *n.* 忧虑

◆ IN THE NAME OF DISCOVERY

Deep in the center of the earth, the main character, Harry, and his uncle, Professor Von Hardwigg, had just discovered a mummy. The mummy *looked to be between thirty and one hundred thousand years old. The bones of prehistoric saber-toothed tigers and other creatures lay all around it. Harry was* apprehensive *about finding living prehistoric people and* mammals*. He feared that he and the professor might be in danger.*

Miguel read more, but the words *jittered* on the page… *"eyes saw really thought did see with immense animals no, under I moving I my gigantic I mighty own about trees… my own."*

The words began to jumble and made little sense to Miguel as he tried to read on. He closed his eyes.

在地心深处，主人公哈里，和他的叔叔冯·哈德维格教授一起，刚刚发现了一具木乃伊。这具木乃伊看起来在三十到十万岁之间。他的周围还有几具史前剑齿虎和其他动物的遗骸。哈里很担心会出现活着的史前人类或者哺乳动物。他害怕教授和他会遇到危险。

米格尔又看了几页，但是，书上的字从书页上跳了出来。

"eyes saw really thought did see with immense animals no, under I moving I my gigantic I mighty own about trees… my own."

米格尔试着读下去，可是，这些字变得杂乱无章，没有任何意义。他闭上了眼睛。

---

mummy *n.* 木乃伊
mammal *n.* 哺乳动物
apprehensive *adj.* 忧虑的
jitter *v.* 紧张不安

ADVENTURE TRIP I

A Giant Discovery

Miguel found upon opening his eyes that the air he was breathing felt thick in his lungs. He knew that from where he had been in the story, in *combination* with the heavy air, that he had been transported to the center of the earth. *Creeping* plants twisted among huge palms and pine trees. *Mosses* and giant ferns blanketed the ground. It was beautiful, except for the fact that everything that should have been green had a faded, brown tint. Even the flowers that should have been all colors of the rainbow were an ugly *beige*.

A voice boomed from behind Miguel, "Of course, Harry! Now come along."

伟大的发现

米格尔一睁开眼睛，就感到他呼入的气体中含有浓重的二氧化碳。他知道，故事中他所在的地方有浓重的二氧化碳，并且他已经被带到了地球的中心。爬行植物缠绕在巨大的棕榈树和松树上。地上覆盖了一层苔藓和蕨类植物。一切看起来都很美，除了本该呈现出绿色的一切都变成了一种淡淡的棕色。甚至连那些本该五颜六色的花朵都变成了丑陋的灰褐色。

一个声音从米格尔身后传来："当然，哈里！快跟过来。"

---

combination *n.* 混合；结合　　　　　　　　creep *v.* 爬行
moss *n.* 苔藓；地衣　　　　　　　　　　　beige *n.* 浅褐色

♦ IN THE NAME OF DISCOVERY

Miguel jumped and turned to see a tall, *skinny* man hurry past him. *That must be the professor, thought Miguel. And I must be Harry, the main character from the book.*

Miguel rushed after the professor, finally catching him as they reached a clearing where an entire herd of *mastodons* stood *grazing* under gigantic palm trees. *Now this is excitement!* thought Miguel, remembering his conversation with Trevon and Lily.

The mastodons appeared to Miguel as hairy, oversized elephants with enormous trunks and *tusks*. Entire trees littered the ground, branches cracked under the mastodons's heavy feet, and leaves rustled as these giants seemed to devour nearly everything in sight.

米格尔吓了一跳，转身看到了一个高高瘦瘦的男人，匆匆地走过他身边。"那一定是教授。"米格尔想，"那么我就是哈里，这本书的主人公。"

米格尔急忙跟在教授身后，终于，在一片空地前追上了他。那里有一整群的乳齿象，他们在巨大的棕榈树下啃着草。"太壮观了！"米格尔想。这时，他想起了他跟特莱文和莉莉的那场对话。

米格尔眼前的这些乳齿象，很像长着毛的、大号的大象，还有长长的鼻子和象牙。整片树林都被连根拔起，树枝被它们巨大的象蹄踏断，树叶

---

skinny *adj.* 极瘦的
graze *v.* 吃青草

mastodon *n.* 乳齿象
tusk *n.* 象牙

ADVENTURE TRIP I

◆ IN THE NAME OF DISCOVERY

Miguel couldn't believe it. He was experiencing an entire *prehistoric* world right in the center of the earth. He wondered if the feelings he was experiencing were the same feelings Drake had felt.

"Let's get closer," said the professor. Miguel hesitated, but the professor pulled him forward.

"We aren't strong enough to battle those prehistoric beasts!" Miguel said. He noticed the wild look in the professor's eyes. It seemed as if the professor was in a *trance*. Professor Von Hardwigg seemed to have lost all reason in his excitement to see, and to be able to get close to, the mastodons.

The professor continued to *inch* forward. "Look, Harry! There's a human being!"

沙沙作响，好像这些庞然大物要毁灭一切。米格尔不敢相信这件事。他正置身于地球中心的一个完完全全的史前世界。他想知道自己现在的感受，是否跟德雷克当时的感受一样。

"我们再走近些。"教授说道。米格尔犹豫了一下，但是教授拉着他向前走。

"我们对付不了这些史前的巨兽！"米格尔说。他注意到教授眼睛里疯狂的眼神，看起来好像教授受了蛊惑。看起来，眼前的景象，能近距离的接触到乳齿象，好像令冯·哈德维格教授失去了理智。

教授继续向前挪动，"看，哈里！那还有一个人！"

prehistoric *adj.* 史前的
inch *v.* 缓慢移动

trance *n.* 昏睡状态

ADVENTURE TRIP I

Miguel saw a giant man who looked twice as tall and as broad as the professor. He was leaning against a *mammoth* tree. Miguel almost lost his breath.

"*Astounding*, my boy, isn't it?" the professor said. "Can you believe it Harry? A living prehistoric man!"

The professor then spoke slowly. "He seems... to be... to be watching the... mastodons." Then Professor Von Hardwigg *roared* with excitement, "He's a mastodon herder! How about that, Harry! We must move closer!"

Miguel's shoulders tensed. The giant human being had some of the features of a man, but his head was the size of a buffalo's. His hair was long like a buffalo's and *matted*. He held a huge tree branch

---

米格尔看到了一个比教授大了一倍的巨人，他正靠在一棵大树上。米格尔吓得大气都不敢出。

"很吓人，孩子，是不是？"教授说，"你能相信吗，哈里？一个活着的史前人类！"

之后，教授慢慢地说："他看起来……好像……好像在看……那些乳齿象。"这时，冯·哈德维格教授激动地喊道："他在放牧乳齿象！怎么样，哈里！我们得再靠近些！"

米格尔缩着肩。这个巨人有人的某些特征，不过，他的头像野牛头一样大。毛发也跟野牛一样，全身上下都是。他手里握着一根大树枝，像是

---

mammoth *adj.* 巨大的
roar *v.* 吼叫

astounding *adj.* 使人震惊的
matted *adj.* 缠结的

◆ IN THE NAME OF DISCOVERY

like a staff.

The professor carefully crept closer.

"Wait," Miguel whispered. The *seriousness* of what they had found had hit him. "You can't *defend* yourself against a giant!"

"I shall chance it," Professor Von Hardwigg said, his eyes wildly *scanning* the creature, "as any true explorer would—this is more incredible than I ever imagined."

"But it isn't worth risking your life," Miguel said to the professor.

"Discovery is worth much more," the professor said, *delirious* with the fever of discovery. "And if I succeed, the entire world will remember that I discovered this ancient man!" As Professor Von Hardwigg stepped forward, a branch broke under his foot.

武器。

教授小心翼翼地向前爬。

"等等，"米格尔小声说。他们的发现可能带来的严重后果吓了他一跳。"你在巨人面前无法保护自己！"

"我要冒险试一下。"冯·哈德维格教授说，他的眼睛睁得大大的，盯着那个生物。"因为任何探险家都会这样做——这比我想象得还要令人难以置信。"

"但是，它不值得你用生命做赌注。"米格尔对教授说。

"发现比生命重要得多。"教授说，发现的兴奋冲昏了他的头。"如果我成功了，全世界都会记得是我发现了这个古代人类！"冯·哈德维格教授在向前走的过程中，脚踩断了一根树枝。

---

seriousness *n.* 严重　　　　　　　　defend *v.* 保护
scan *v.* 细看；端详　　　　　　　　delirious *adj.* 极兴奋的

ADVENTURE TRIP 1

The giant was *startled* and looked up at them.

Miguel *scrunched* his eyes as if closing them would hide both explorers from the giant's sight.

Captured!

A loud *grunt* came from across the clearing as the giant pulled himself to his full height, pointing his staff in their direction.

"He looks as if he's warning us to stay away," said Miguel.

"Not to worry," the professor said, rounding his shoulders forward and lowering his gaze. "I am no threat to him."

The mastodons *stomped* and trumpeted. "Turn back," Miguel shouted. Professor Von Hardwigg waved him away as he moved toward the giant.

巨人吓了一跳，朝他们的方向看来。

米格尔闭上了眼睛。好像闭上眼睛，他们两个就不会被巨人发现了似的。

成为俘虏！

从空地那边传来了一声吼叫，巨人站起来，用树枝指着他们的方向。

"他看起来好像在警告我们离开。"米格尔说。

"不用担心。"教授说着低下头，缩着肩膀继续往前走。"我威胁不到他。"

那些乳齿象迈着重重的步子走，吼叫着。"回来。"米格尔喊。冯·

---

startled *adj.* 受惊吓的
grunt *n.* 呼噜声

scrunch *v.* 挤压；扭曲
stomp *v.* 迈着重重的步子走

◆ IN THE NAME OF DISCOVERY

The giant stepped forward, too, *thrashing* his staff in the air. The professor *crouched* lower as if to hide, but the giant advanced quickly toward him.

"Watch out, professor!" Miguel shouted.

In an instant, the giant *scooped up* the professor and tossed him over his shoulder like a sack of potatoes. The giant raised his staff and howled with victory. He *pivoted* back toward the mastodon herd and retreated into the woods.

"The greatest adventure yet!" the professor yelled before disappearing into the trees.

Professor Von Hardwigg had been captured just like a fly in a spider's web. Miguel's thoughts blurred. There must be a way to save him! Miguel took off running toward the giant even though his

---

哈德维格教授一边向前走，一边向他挥手。

那个巨人也向前走了几步，在空中舞动着他的树枝。教授蹲下了身子，好像要藏起来，但是，巨人向他快步走过来。

"小心，教授！"米格尔喊。

顷刻间，巨人来到了教授身边，像扛土豆一样，一下子把他扛到肩上。巨人举起树枝，发出了胜利的吼叫。他转身朝象群走去，走进了森林。

"这仍然是最伟大的探险！"教授喊着，消失在了树林中。

冯·哈德维格教授被抓住了，就像一只困在蜘蛛网里的苍蝇。米格尔

---

thrash *v.* （使）激烈扭动　　　　crouch *v.* 蹲下
scoop up 抱起　　　　　　　　　　pivot *v.* （使）在枢轴上转动

ADVENTURE TRIP I

body was trembling with fear. Here he was, stuck in another world, in the center of the earth, with no way out.

What would the giant do to the professor? Was he a prisoner or, like the spider's *prey*, the giant's next meal? There was no time to find out. "Think, Miguel, think!"

"I know! Hans!" Miguel shouted. "I have to remember where Hans is at this point in the book. I have to find him and get help. Think, Miguel!" Then Miguel heard his dad reading the story from last year as if it were happening right then and he knew—Hans would be at the beach with the *raft*.

Miguel ran past the clearing, jumping over rushing *brooks*. Even though the *hollow* eyes of the mummy sent chills down Miguel's neck, he ran past it, through the cemetery of scattered bones. No

---

吓糊涂了。一定有办法救他！米格尔尽管吓得浑身发抖，还是朝着巨人跑过去。他现在置身于另一个世界，在地球中心，想不出解决的办法。

那个巨人会怎么对待教授？会囚禁他吗？还是像蜘蛛的猎物一样，成为巨人的美味？没有时间去一探究竟。"快想办法，米格尔，好好想想！"

"我想到了！汉斯！"米格尔叫道，"我得想一下，书里的汉斯现在在什么地方。我得找到他，让他帮忙。好好想想，米格尔！"然后，米格尔的耳边响起了去年父亲读这本书的声音，他知道——汉斯应该在岸边的木筏上。

米格尔跑过空地，跳过流淌的溪水。尽管木乃伊空洞的眼睛吓得他脊背发直，他还是跑了过去，他也跑过了那些散落一地的残骸。没有时间停

---

prey *n.* 猎物
brook *n.* 小溪

raft *n.* 木筏
hollow *adj.* 空的；空洞的

◆ IN THE NAME OF DISCOVERY

time to stop and think about being scared. He just had to push on and get help.

A Two-Man Band

Miguel's feet moved forward, down great walls of *speckled* and *crystallized* rock. Once down the slopes, he raced across a white beach made of thousands of shells—the shells *crunching* and *sliding* under his feet. "I can hear the ocean!" he said aloud, almost colliding with an empty turtle shell the size of the beanbag chair in his bedroom.

Suddenly a large body of water appeared before him, spreading out as far as he could see. Huge, gray swells, louder than a fleet of jet engines, erupted a few hundred yards offshore. In the distance,

---

下来，也没有时间害怕。他必须奋力向前奔跑，找人帮忙。

两个人的乐队

米格尔继续向前跑，顺着斑驳的晶化岩石墙体，一直向下跑。跑下了山坡，经过了一片上千只贝壳构成的白色海滩。这些贝壳在他的脚下不断地爬来爬去。"我能听见大海了！"他大声地说，差点没撞到一个空龟壳，这个龟壳几乎跟他卧室里的豆椅一样大。

突然间，他的眼前出现了一片水，一望无际。巨大的灰色海浪，比一

---

speckled adj. 布满斑点的　　　　crystallized adj. 结晶的
crunch v. 嘎吱嘎吱地动　　　　　slide v. （使）快捷而悄声地移动

ADVENTURE TRIP I

Miguel spotted a man working around what looked like a *battered* raft.

Hans barely looked up from his repair work when Miguel approached him. Out of breath, Miguel *panted*, "The professor's in trouble! He's been captured!"

Hans stared up blankly. "He needs our help!" continued Miguel. "Come on!"

Then Miguel remembered that Hans didn't speak English, so he *motioned* for the man to follow him. Once in the woods, Miguel listened for the mastodons, but all he heard was silence. A *lump* grew in his throat. *What if he was too late?*

队快艇的声音还要大，在距离海岸几百码的地方翻滚。在远处，米格尔看到了一个在破旧的木筏附近干活的人。

　　米格尔走进汉斯的时候，他头也不抬地在修船。米格尔气喘吁吁地说："教授遇到麻烦了！他被抓住了！"

　　汉斯愣愣地看着他。"他需要我们的帮助！"米格尔继续说，"走啊！"

　　这时，米格尔想起了汉斯不懂英语。于是，他用手势告诉汉斯跟他走。一走进树林，米格尔就仔细倾听，想找到那些乳齿象，可他什么也没听见。他的心提到了嗓子眼儿。要是他来得太晚了，怎么办？

---

battered *adj.* 破旧的
motion *v.* 打手势

pant *v.* 气喘；喘息
lump *n.* 喉咙哽住；哽咽

◆ IN THE NAME OF DISCOVERY

Hans picked up on Miguel's anxiety and crept silently through the *ferns*, now keeping Miguel behind him. Though he didn't speak English, he seemed to understand what was happening from Miguel's body language. A loud trumpeting sound *blasted* through the air. Miguel and Hans froze. The mastodons! Miguel reasoned that the professor had to be near! Hopefully he was still alive.

Hans and Miguel followed the sound of the animals until it grew quiet. Then Miguel's ears picked up on something he had not heard before—a quiet tapping. He listened closely. It was Morse code! Dash-dash-dot. Dot-dot. Dot-dash. Miguel had learned Morse code at summer camp. "The professor must be sending a message!" he said. Miguel closed his eyes and *decoded* the taps. G-I-A-N-T A-F-R-

汉斯感觉到了米格尔的担心，轻轻地爬过那些蕨类植物，现在，他已经爬到米格尔的前面了。虽然不懂英语，可是他好像已经从米格尔的身体语言中，知道了发生的事情。一个响亮的声音回荡在空中，米格尔和汉斯停在了那里。是那些乳齿象！米格尔知道教授应该就在附近！祈祷着他还活着。

汉斯和米格尔循着那个声音，一直走，直到周围静了下来。这时，米格尔听到了一些他以前没听到过的声音——轻轻的敲击声。他凑近仔细听了听。是莫尔斯密码！嗒嗒嘀，嘀嘀，嘀嗒。米格尔在夏令营的时候学过莫尔斯密码。"教授一定在传递消息！"他说。米格尔闭上了眼睛，破译着密码。巨人 害怕 噪音 救命

fern *n.* 蕨类植物
decode *v.* 解（码）

blast *v.* 轰鸣

ADVENTURE TRIP I

A-I-D L-O-U-D N-O-I-S-E-S H-E-L-P

Gears shifted in Miguel's brain as the professor kept repeating the message. "That's it!" Miguel jumped up. He *flashed back* to school and what he had learned about Sir Francis Drake. Drake had become an expert at *toppling* Spanish colonies and stealing anything of value that he could find. He did this by playing a trick on the colonists. He would have his crew make lots of noise to make the colonists think there were more members to his crew than there actually were.

"We need to make lots of noise so the giant thinks we are an enormous group of *warriors*," screamed Miguel, forgetting that Hans couldn't understand him. He then motioned to Hans that they needed to get back to the beach.

教授重复地发送信息，米格尔不停地转动着脑筋。"就这些！"米格尔跳了起来。他的思绪回到了学校，想起了他学到的关于弗朗西斯·德雷克爵士的故事。德雷克专门劫持西班牙殖民者，抢夺他们的财物。他总是通过一些计谋打败这些殖民者。他会吩咐手下制造出很大的声音，让殖民者们以为他们有比实际多得多的大批人马。

"我们需要制造出许多声音，让巨人以为我们是一队勇士。"米格尔叫道，忘记了汉斯听不懂他的话。然后，他用手势告诉汉斯他们需要返回海滩。

---

gear　*n.*　齿轮
topple　*v.*　推翻；颠覆

flash back　回忆；回想
warrior　*n.*　勇士

◆ IN THE NAME OF DISCOVERY

Back at the beach, Miguel had Hans *stack* and carry two large turtle shells. Hans picked up a *conch* shell the size of a turkey and blew into it, producing a sound like a bass tuba.

"Great idea!" Miguel said. "We'll be a two-man band and rock-and-roll this giant until he's scared to death!"

Hans picked up some heavy sticks to use as *drumsticks* against the two large shells. Miguel found a conch shell of his own and then strung together a line of smaller turtle shells with a vine. He tied the string of turtle shells around his waist, and then he and Hans headed back to find the grazing mastodons and, hopefully, the giant and the professor.

It wasn't long before they found the giant *stooping* over a

回到海滩，米格尔让汉斯找来了两个大龟壳。汉斯拾起一个龟壳大小的海螺壳，吹了起来。产生了一种像大号一样的声音。

"好主意！"米格尔说。"我们要组成一支二人乐队，吓唬那个巨人，吓死他！"

汉斯捡了一些棍子，用来作为敲打龟壳的鼓棒。米格尔也为自己找了一个海螺壳，然后又用绳子串起一串小龟壳，系在腰间。然后，他和汉斯就回去寻找那些放牧的乳齿象了，希望能通过它们，找到巨人和教授。

没过多久，他们就找到了篝火旁边的巨人。教授就在他身边，被巨人用藤条捆在了树桩上。米格尔展开了行动，汉斯也学着他的样子，做了起

---

stack *v.* 堆起来   conch *n.* 海螺
drumstick *n.* 鼓棒   stoop *v.* （站立或行走时）弓背

ADVENTURE TRIP I

campfire. Nearby, the professor was *staked* to the ground with vines. Miguel went into action, and Hans followed suit. Miguel *flipped* the turtle shells over, grabbed a stick and began to drum across the tops of the shells. Hans lifted his conch shell and began blowing as loud as he could.

Along with the horn and the drums, Miguel began to scream the first song that popped into his head. "WE WILL, WE WILL, ROCK YOU …"

The giant immediately stood *erect*. His eyes darted about the forest.

" … WE WILL, WE WILL, ROCK YOU!" Bang, bang, honk, honk! The mastodons roared and so did the giant.

来。米格尔把那些龟壳翻过来，抓起木棍，开始击打龟壳背面。汉斯举起海螺壳，用力地吹。

随着鼓声和号声，米格尔高声唱出他头脑中出现的第一首歌。"我们，我们，要打败你……"

巨人立即站直了身体，他用眼睛打量着森林。

"我们，我们，要打败你……"梆梆，轰轰！

乳齿象被吓坏了，巨人也被吓坏了。

---

stake *v.* 用桩支撑
erect *adj.* 直立地

flip *v.* （使）快速翻转

◆ IN THE NAME OF DISCOVERY

"Keep it up, boy!" shouted the professor.

"…WE WILL, WE WILL, ROCK YOU!"

Upon Miguel's last verse, trees and bushes bent and cracked in opposite directions as the mastodons took off—the giant running close behind them.

"You've done it!" the professor cheered. "You've scared away the *mighty* beasts!"

Miguel rushed over to the professor. "You're safe!" he cried.

"Thanks to you and Hans!" the professor said. "Now *untie* my bonds, Harry, before that giant returns!"

Miguel glanced around in hopes of finding a stone tool or weapon

---

"接着唱，孩子！"教授喊道。

"……我们，我们，要打败你！"

米格尔的声音一落，树枝都向相反的方向倾倒，断裂。因为乳齿象抬起腿，逃跑了——巨人紧跟在它们后面。

"你们成功了！"教授欢呼道，"你们吓跑了巨兽！"

米格尔连忙跑到教授身边。"您安全了！"他喊道。

"谢谢你和汉斯！"教授说。"快点解开藤条，哈里，趁巨人没回来！"

米格尔环顾四周，希望能找到石片或是武器，这时，他想起了口袋里

---

mighty *adj.* 巨大的　　　　　　　　　　untie *v.* 解开

ADVENTURE TRIP I

when he remembered what he had in his pocket. He gently pulled out the *dagger* he'd found on the Great Gallardo's chest and cut the palm twine that held the professor down. A *lightbulb* clicked on inside Miguel's head. *It's like the book knows what I'll need to make things right!*

Professor Von Hardwigg bear-hugged Miguel. "You were right, Harry," Professor Von Hardwigg said. "Nothing is worth risking our lives, not even the most *astonishing* discovery. Let's go home."

Home sounded wonderful. Miguel handed the dagger to the professor. "Here is something you can take home with you."

"Is that what I think it is?" the professor *gasped*. "Could it be the

的匕首。他从口袋里掏出在伟大的盖拉多的箱子里发现的那个匕首，割断了那个捆着教授的棕榈藤。这时候，米格尔的头脑中突然闪过一个想法。"那本书好像知道我一定会用到这把匕首！"

冯·哈德维格教授紧紧地拥抱了米格尔。"你说得对，哈里。"教授说，"没用什么值得我们用生命去冒险，即使是最惊人的发现。我们回家吧。"

回家听起来很美好。米格尔把匕首递给教授。"你可以把这个一起带回家。"

"这是真的吗？"教授问道。"是第一个到达地心的探险家——安·

dagger *n.* 匕首
astonishing *adj.* 惊人的

lightbulb *n.* 电灯泡
gasp *v.* 气喘吁吁地说

◆ IN THE NAME OF DISCOVERY

famous dagger of Arne Saknussemm, the first explorer to reach the center of the earth?" Hans looked at the dagger in *awe* at the mention of the fellow Icelander's name.

As Miguel let go of the dagger, he closed his eyes. In seconds, a cool breeze met him back at the loft, safe and sound.

Miguel breathed a sigh of relief. Now he had *witnessed* first-hand how dangerous and *overwhelming* the power of discovery could be. Explorers were brave and smart, but often blinded by the *perceived* glory of their discovery. Miguel was glad he'd saved the professor, but for now, Miguel was content to discover each day of his own life—right here and right now, with, of course, a little help from the Great Gallardo's books every now and then!

沙克纳塞姆，那把著名的匕首吗？"听到提到那个冰岛人的名字后，汉斯敬畏地看着那把匕首。

米格尔给出匕首后，闭上了眼睛。几秒钟后，他感到一阵凉风吹过，他安全地回到了阁楼。

米格尔大大地出了一口气。现在他已经亲眼看见了发现所带来的危险了，无法抗拒的吸引力。探险者十分聪明勇敢，但是，他们经常会被发现所带来的荣誉蒙蔽了双眼。米格尔很高兴他能救出教授，不过，现在米格尔对自己每天的生活中的新发现很满意。当然，有时需要借助伟大的盖拉多的魔法书的帮助！

---

awe *n.* 敬畏
overwhelming *adj.* 势不可挡的

witness *v.* 见证
perceive *v.* 察觉到

ADVENTURE TRIP I

06

Atlantic Crossing

Leaving Dublin Bay

Patrick Kelley looked out over the ships floating in Dublin *Bay*. Below him, he saw hundreds of people crowding the docks, looking for space on one of the ships *bound for* America. The year was 1846, and many Irish people, most of whom were farmers, were *starving*. For the past two years, Ireland's potato crop had failed due to disease, resulting in a great *famine*.

横渡大西洋

离开都柏林港湾

帕特里克·凯利向远处看去,他看到了停泊在都柏林港湾的那些船。在他身下,好几百人挤在码头上,在某艘开往美国的船上,寻找着属于他们的位子。这一年是1846年,许多爱尔兰人饱受饥饿之苦,他们中的大部分人都是农民。在过去的两年里,因为病害,爱尔兰的土豆作物颗粒无收,造成了严重的饥荒。

---

bay *n.* 湾
starve *v.* 挨饿
bound for 准备前往(某地)
famine *n.* 饥荒

◆ ATLANTIC CROSSING

To avoid *starvation*, Irish families like Patrick's bought passage on ships of all sizes sailing to the United States and Canada. The journey was dangerous, but the promise of a better life in America, where there was more land to farm and no diseases destroying the crops, drew many to the *harbor*. Patrick heard his father talk of jobs in big cities like New York and Boston. His father, who was a *blacksmith*, hoped to find a job working his craft in New York, which had thousands of horses to pull carriages and *wagons* through the streets. For that much work, Patrick's father was ready to leave Ireland.

Patrick knew his family was suffering, and he knew that America might offer a better life, yet Patrick did not want to leave Dublin. This

---

为了逃避饥荒，许多跟帕特里克家一样的爱尔兰家庭，购买了船票，前往美国和加拿大。尽管危险重重，但是美国美好的生活前景还是吸引了大量的移民。那里有广阔的无人耕种的土地，没有危害庄稼的病害。帕特里克听父亲说起过纽约和波士顿这样的大城市里有很多工作。他的父亲是个铁匠，希望能够在纽约找到一个类似的工作。纽约的街道上有数千辆载人和运货的马车。为了那么多的工作机会，帕特里克的父亲已经做好了离开爱尔兰的准备。

帕特里克了解他的家庭正经历苦难，也知道美国可能会为他们提供更好的生活，但他仍然不想离开都柏林。这里是他的家，他不想离开朋友

---

starvation *n.* 饥饿　　　　　　　　　　　harbor *n.* 港口
blacksmith *n.* 铁匠　　　　　　　　　　wagon *n.* 四轮载重马车

ADVENTURE TRIP I

was his home. He did not want to leave his friends, despite the food shortage, and he did not want to leave Dublin Bay, his favorite place. He often sat on the shore overlooking the bay during storms and felt the sea *spray* in his face, and he would listen to the stories of the *suntanned* sailors returning from journeys all around the world.

Patrick wanted to be a sailor in the warm South Pacific Ocean; he did not want to be a crowded passenger aboard an *immigrant* ship crossing the cold Atlantic.

So, Patrick sat on the docks by himself, angry with his family, mostly his father, for making him leave. He shaded his eyes from the setting sun on the *horizon* and looked for the tall mast of the *Donegal*, the ship that would take his family to America the following morning.

们，他也不想离开都柏林港湾，这里是他最喜欢的地方。他总是坐在岸边，眺望着暴风雨中的港湾，任由海上飞沫扑打在他的脸上，聆听世界各地返航的饱经风霜的水手讲述旅程中的故事。

帕特里克想成为一名水手，在温暖的南太平洋上航行；不想变成簇拥在移民船甲板上的乘客，在寒冷的大西洋上穿行。

所以，帕特里克独自一人坐在码头上，生着家人的气。他尤其生父亲的气，因为他迫使自己离开这儿。他用手遮着眼睛，在地平线上落日的余晖中，寻找多尼哥号的高高的桅杆。这条船将在明天早上，带着他们一家前往美国。他在码头不远处看到了多尼哥号，它很显眼，因为它比大多

---

spray n. 浪花
immigrant n. 移民

suntanned adj. 晒得黝黑的
horizon n. 地平线

◆ ATLANTIC CROSSING

He spotted the *Donegal* a little farther down the docks; it was easy to pick out because it was larger than most of the other ships. He could see the name painted in gold letters across the *stern* of the ship as it gently *bobbed in* the water. Patrick glared at the massive boat, wishing it would sink to the bottom of Dublin Bay. He shut his eyes, closing out the sight.

Promise of a Better Life

By the time Patrick finally decided to go home, it had grown dark. Patrick lived on the edge of Dublin, where his house was connected to his father's large blacksmith barn and shop. After he left the edge of the water, which reflected the oil lamps along the docks and the faint moonlight above, the streets and alleyways leading home were

---

数船都要大。它静静地浮在水面上，他能看到船尾处用金色的漆喷涂的名字。帕特里克凝视着这只巨轮，祈祷它会沉入都柏林港湾的水底。他闭上眼睛，不再看它。

美好生活的希望

帕特里克最终决定回家的时候，天已经黑了。帕特里克住在都柏林的边上，他的家挨着父亲打铁的仓库和铺子。他离开了水边，水面上倒映着码头上的油灯和天上发着淡淡光亮的月亮。通往他家的大街小巷都很暗，

---

stern *n.* 船尾　　　　　　　　　　　　　　　　　bob in 进入

ADVENTURE TRIP 1

so dark that he could see just a short way ahead. The dim *glow* coming from the windows of houses did little to light his way.

After a few *blocks*, Patrick noticed footsteps behind him. The streets were usually deserted after dark, and Patrick wondered who might be out tonight. The footsteps drew closer and closer, and as he listened, Patrick *detected* a strange *metallic* clicking along with the footsteps. Frightened, Patrick kept his head down and began walking faster.

Another block later, the steps and the clicking got closer still. Frantically, Patrick tried to remember an alleyway or doorway he could duck into to get away from this stranger following him.

Suddenly, Patrick felt a small jab on the top of his shoulder. His

---

他只能看见前面很短的距离。各家各户窗子里透出的微弱光亮也不能使他看清前面的路。

走了几个街区后，帕特里克注意到了身后的脚步声。天黑之后，通常街道上不会有什么行人，帕特里克想谁会在今天晚上出门呢。脚步声越来越近了，仔细一听，帕特里克听出了脚步声中还夹杂着一种奇怪的金属点击地面的声音。帕特里克吓坏了，低下头，加快了脚步。

又过了一个街区后，脚步声和金属声更近了。帕特里克疯狂地想找个小巷或者门洞，钻进去，摆脱这个跟踪他的陌生人。

突然间，帕特里克感到有人轻轻地拍了一下他的肩膀。他吓得全身

---

glow n. 暗淡的光　　　　　　　　　　block n. 街区
detect v. 发现　　　　　　　　　　　metallic adj. 金属般的

◆ ATLANTIC CROSSING

blood froze in terror.

"Excuse me, young man!" he heard behind him. Patrick stood still, afraid to turn around.

"Young man, I say! Where are you off to? I noticed you eyeing the *Donegal* down at the docks."

Still frightened, Patrick slowly turned around. Standing over him glared an older man with a silver beard glowing in the *lamplight* and a military sword in his right hand.

"Who are you?" Patrick asked, trying to sound confident.

"I am First Mate Thomas O'Brien, an officer of the *Donegal*, at your service," he answered in a serious *tone*.

"The *Donegal*?" Patrick repeated. "My family and I are sailing on

血液都凝固了。

"打扰一下，年轻人！"从他身后传来了一个声音。帕特里克站在那里一动不动，不敢转身。

"年轻人，我说！你要去哪儿？我看到你在码头上一直盯着多尼哥号。"

帕特里克仍然很害怕，慢慢地转过身来。他借着灯光，看到身旁有一个白胡子老人，右手拿着一把军剑。

"你是谁？"帕特里克强作镇定地问。

"我是多尼哥号上的军官，托马斯·奥布莱恩大副。"他一本正经地回答。

"多尼哥号？"帕特里克重复道，"我和家人明天就要乘坐多尼哥

lamplight *n.* 灯光   tone *n.* 语气

ADVENTURE TRIP I

the *Donegal* tomorrow."

"Ah, very good," O'Brien answered. "She's a fine ship, and the sailing conditions are better than most other ships these days."

"But I hear the living conditions are bad on these ships," Patrick asked.

"Well, they often are," Thomas replied. "Some ships are worse than others. Unfortunately, conditions usually depend upon how much money a family can spend on their *fare*."

"Yeah, I know," Patrick *interrupted*. "My father spent most of our savings on this trip."

"Your family will travel on a ship with a record for bringing its passengers safely to America, even though the journey will still be

---

号。"

"啊，非常好。"奥布莱恩回答，"它是一艘好船，跟这年头的大多数船比，它的航行条件很好。"

"但是，我听说这些船上的生活条件很差。"帕特里克说。

"是的，这些船经常是这样。"托马斯回答，"一些船还要更差劲。不幸的是，条件通常取决于一个家庭能承担多少钱的船票。"

"是的，我知道。"帕特里克插嘴说，"我父亲为了这次航行，花掉了我们大部分的积蓄。"

"你们一家搭乘的是一艘创造了纪录的船。尽管旅途中会有些困难和

---

fare *n.* 船费　　　　　　　　　　　　　　interrupt *v.* 打断

◆ ATLANTIC CROSSING

difficult and uncomfortable," O'Brien said. "The Atlantic is a huge ocean, and the weather can be dangerous on the open sea."

Patrick thought about this for a moment. "I can't remember the last time I wasn't going to bed feeling hungry. I don't want to live like that much longer."

"Exactly," Thomas responded. "In an *emergency*, people must make difficult choices to make life better. But listen to me, young man. I've seen America many times, and I think that a better life is waiting for you and your family. You will have to work very hard, but if you do, there should be no limit to what you can *accomplish*."

"Yes, sir. That's what my dad keeps telling me. Maybe he's right," Patrick *admitted*.

不舒服，它带着所有的乘客安全地抵达了美国。" 奥布莱恩说，"大西洋水域广阔，海面上的多变的天气可能会带来一定的危险。"

帕特里克想了一会儿说："我想不起来，上一次不饿着肚皮睡觉是什么时候了。我不想再过这样的日子了。"

"太对了。"托马斯回应道。"在一些特殊的情况下，人们必须做出艰难的选择，谋求更好的生活。但是，听我说，年轻人。我去过美国很多次了，我想那里有更好的生活等着你和你的家人。你们需要努力地工作，但是如果你们这样做了，就一定会获得意想不到的收获。"

"是的，先生，我父亲就是一直这样告诉我的。也许他是对的。"帕特里克认同地说。

---

emergency n. 紧急情况　　　　　　　　　accomplish v. 完成
admit v. 承认

ADVENTURE TRIP I

"Of course he's right, son," Thomas answered. He then looked back toward the harbor. "Well, young man, it's getting late. You should be off to bed. After all, this may be the last peaceful night's sleep you'll have for several weeks," he said with a *wink*.

"Okay, sir. Thank you for the advice. Maybe I'll see you on the ship," Patrick said as he turned to go home.

Stormy Seas

A week later, Patrick and his family were well on their way to America *aboard* the *Donegal*.

"All hands on deck! All hands on *deck*!" Patrick heard from above. In the darkness below decks, Patrick heard his sister groaning. She had been sick for three days, like many of the people on the ship.

"他当然是对的，孩子。"托马斯答道。然后，他回过头，看着海港。"好了，年轻人，天已经很黑了。你应该回去睡觉了。毕竟，这也许会是几个星期内，你睡得最好的一夜了。"他眨了眨眼说。

"好的，先生。谢谢你的建议。也许我会在船上看见你。"帕特里克说着转过身，向家走去。

狂风暴雨中的大海

一周后，帕特里克和家人已经登上了多尼哥号，在去往美国的途中了。

"全体人员都上甲板！全体人员都上甲板！"帕特里克听到上面在

---

wink *n.* 眨眼示意   aboard *adv.* 在（船上）
deck *n.* 甲板

◆ ATLANTIC CROSSING

After several days of calm seas sailing from Dublin, the *Donegal* had run into a violent storm.

On the first day of the storm, Patrick watched from the deck with excitement as giant walls of water would *swell* and approach the ship. Patrick's stomach would rise in his throat as the *Donegal* climbed, *hovered* for one awful second at the *crest* of the wave, then crashed down the far side of the wave in a great rush.

This was exciting, but the storm was getting stronger, and the constant rising and falling of the ship was *churning* the stomachs of the passengers, many of whom, like Patrick's sister, became seasick.

"All hands on deck! We must lower these sails, boys!" Patrick

喊。在黑暗的船舱里，帕特里克听到姐姐在呻吟。跟船上的许多人一样，她已经病了三天了。从都柏林出发后，他们在平静的海面上，航行了几天。然后，多尼哥号就遇上了猛烈的暴风雨。

第一天遭遇暴风雨的时候，帕特里克兴奋地从甲板上望向海面。他看见一排排巨浪从海面升起，翻滚着向他们的船袭来。他总是提心吊胆地看着多尼哥号爬上巨浪，在浪尖上盘旋一会儿，然后猛地一下，冲到了浪底。

这个时候很令人激动，但是暴风雨越来越猛烈，船不断地上下摇动。搅动着乘客们的胃，许多人都像帕特里克的姐姐一样，晕船了。

"全体人员都上甲板！我们必须把这些帆降下来，伙计们！" 帕特

swell *v.* 鼓出；凸出	hover *v.* 盘旋
crest *n.* 浪尖	churn *v.* 剧烈搅动

ADVENTURE TRIP I

heard these commands again from above. He knew that "hands" only meant the sailors, not any of the passengers, but he felt he couldn't stand staying below in the darkness one more moment. He *desperately* wanted to see the sailors handling the stormy conditions. So, when no one was looking, Patrick burst up the main *hatch* and into the *howling* wind and freezing spray.

The deck of the ship was wildly confusing—sailors running around, officers barking orders, sails flapping in the wind, and white ocean spray crashing over the rails of the ship.

"Captain! One of the sails has wrapped itself around the upper yardarm!" Patrick heard a sailor yell out to the captain.

"Well, send someone up there to *untangle* it. We need that sail

---

里克又听到了上面发出的命令。他知道，"人员"指的是海员，不是乘客。但是，他感到他不能再待在黑漆漆的下面了，连一分钟也不能待了。他非常想看看水手们是如何与暴风雨对抗的。于是，趁着没人注意，帕特里克爬上了主舱口，站在了呼啸的海风和冰冷的海上飞沫中。

甲板上异常混乱——水手们跑来跑去，长官们发号着施令，船帆在风中拍打着桅杆，白色的海上飞沫冲撞着船上的围栏。

"船长！一个帆缠在了上面的横桅上！" 帕特里克听到一个水手向船长大喊。

"那么，派个人上去，把它解开。风把它撕碎前，我们得把那个帆降

---

desperately *adv.* 极其；非常　　　　　　　　　　hatch *n.* 舱
howl *v.* 呼啸；怒号　　　　　　　　　　　　　　untangle *v.* 解开

◆ ATLANTIC CROSSING

down before the wind tears it!" the captain thundered.

"We can't, sir," the sailor replied. "The *yardarm* has been damaged in the wind and can't support a sailor's weight. We would need someone much smaller."

The sailors hadn't noticed Patrick yet, but as he heard this, he only needed to think about what they said for a moment.

"Excuse me, sir!" he said as he *tugged* on the captain's coat. The captain turned quickly and, seeing Patrick, yelled, "You, boy! What are you doing above deck? Get yourself below with the other passengers."

"But, sir," Patrick protested. "I can climb the *mast* and untangle the sail."

"What? You? What makes you think you could do this? It's

下来！"船长高声喊道。

"我们办不到，先生。"水手回答，"横桁被风吹裂了，它支撑不住一个水手的重量。我们需要找一个小孩。"

水手们仍然没注意帕特里克，但是，听到这儿，他想了一下他们的对话。

"请问，先生！"他拽了一下船长的衣服说。船长迅速地转过身来，看见了帕特里克，大叫："是你，孩子！你在甲板上干什么？快下去，跟其他的乘客待在一起。"

"可是，先生，"帕特里克抗议道，"我可以爬上桅杆，解开船帆。"

"什么？你？你凭什么认为自己可以做到？外面风很大，不是乘客待

---

yardarm *n.* 帆桁端
mast *n.* 桅杆

tug *v.* 拽

ADVENTURE TRIP I

howling out here. These are no conditions for a passenger."

"It's really no problem, sir. I've grown up along the coast all my life. The wind doesn't bother me, and I have to climb in the *rafters* of my father's blacksmith barn every day to hang up his tools." Patrick said this with as much confidence as he could fake, but the wild wind and water frightened him. He didn't dare to actually look up at the mast.

Before the captain could answer, another sailor interrupted them.

"Sir, we must do something quickly, the sail is beginning to tear!"

The captain looked out over the stormy sea, then leaned down and grabbed Patrick by the shoulders. "All right, lad. Be careful, climb slowly, and do not look down. Just *concentrate* on the mast ahead of you. You can do this! Now, up you go."

的地方。"

"真的没问题，先生。我一直在海边长大。狂风影响不了我，我每天都要爬到爸爸的铁匠仓库的椽子上，把他的工具挂上。" 帕特里克装出自信的样子说。但是，狂风巨浪令他胆怯了，他不敢抬头看桅杆。

没等船长回答，另一个水手上前打断他们说：

"先生，我们必须快点，船帆要被风撕裂了！"

船长抬头望了一眼暴风雨中的海面，然后，低下头，抓着帕特里克的肩膀说："好吧，孩子。小心点，慢点爬，千万不要往下看。盯着你面前的桅杆。你一定能行！现在，上去吧。"

---

rafter *n.* 椽子　　　　　　　　concentrate *v.* 集中注意力

◆ ATLANTIC CROSSING

Climbing the mast wasn't scary for Patrick at first, as long as he just looked straight ahead. Halfway up, however, Patrick was unable to resist *temptation* and, holding tightly to the mast, he looked out and below him.

Through a *crisscross* of ropes whistling in the wind, he saw the white tops of the waves surrounding the ship and the small heads of the sailors *scurrying* around the deck of the ship. He briefly thought of his family out of sight below the deck, and how worried his mother would be right now if she saw him up here. This thought vanished quickly, however, as Patrick felt a wave of *dizziness* overtake him. The rocking of the ship on the waves was twice as strong up on the mast, and seeing all the waves around him made his head spin.

一开始，爬在桅杆上并没有吓到帕特里克，只要他一直盯着上面。然而，上到一半时，帕特里克紧紧地抓着桅杆，禁不住向下看了一眼。

透过在风中摇动着的交错的绳索，他看到了船周围的白色的浪尖，还有在甲板上跑来跑去的水手的头顶。他一下子想到了甲板下的家人，如果妈妈此时看到他在桅杆上，该多担心啊。不过，帕特里克这时感到一阵眩晕，这些想法很快就消失了。船在大浪中剧烈地摇晃，比桅杆上面摇晃的要剧烈两倍。看到周围的巨浪，他感到一阵眩晕向他袭来。克制住眩晕，

---

temptation *n.* 诱惑　　　　　　　crisscross *adj.* 纵横交错的
scurry *v.* 急奔　　　　　　　　　dizziness *n.* 眩晕

ADVENTURE TRIP I

Fighting against this dizziness, Patrick refocused on the mast in front of him. His head quickly cleared, and he climbed the rest of the way up the mast.

At the top, he could see the *crack* in the wood of the yardarm, but it didn't look very large, so he knew if he took care, he would be okay. Looking out, he could see the top of the sail *flapping* in the wind and the clip he needed to *unhook* to lower the sail.

"Okay," he said to himself. "Here goes."

Carefully reaching out from the mast, Patrick stretched his hand toward the clip. Glancing down for a moment, he could see the faces of the captain and crew looking up at him from below. Stretching a bit farther, feeling the mast *sway* dangerously under him, he caught

---

帕特里克重新专注地看着前面的桅杆。他的头脑很快就清醒了，沿着桅杆一直爬到了杆顶。

在杆顶，他看到了横桅上的裂缝。不过，看起来并不十分严重。他知道，如果自己小心一点，一定不会有什么问题。向远处望去，他看到了帆的顶端正在风中拍打着桅杆，也看到了船帆被夹住的地方，他需要解开那儿，把帆降下来。

"好了。"他对自己说，"上去吧。"

帕特里克从桅杆上小心翼翼地伸出手，伸向帆被夹住的地方。他向下瞟了一眼，看到船长和船员们都在下面仰着脸看着他。帕特里克又向前伸了一

---

crack *n.* 断裂   flap *v.* 拍打
unhook *v.* 解开（衣物等）的钩子   sway *v.* 摇晃

◆ ATLANTIC CROSSING

ADVENTURE TRIP 1

hold of the clip. Tugging with all of the strength he could find in his *awkward* position, he felt the clip give way and the sail drop below him. A cheer rose from the sailors below, and the captain happily waved at him to come back down the mast.

Arriving in America

Three weeks later, Patrick stood on the deck of the *Donegal* with his family. Before them the buildings of New York City came into view. At last, they had made it to America! On the docks, Patrick could see the activity as other ships were unloading from their own ocean journeys. Patrick could feel the energy and *bustle* of this new, growing city, so different from the centuries-old calmness of Dublin.

点。感到身下的桅杆摇晃地更猛烈了。他一把抓住了被夹住的帆，战战兢兢地使出全身的力气使劲地拉了一下，帆一下子解开了，落到了他身下。下面的水手一下子欢呼起来，船长高兴地向他挥手，让他从桅杆上下来。

抵达美国

三周后，帕特里克和家人一起站在多尼哥号的甲板上，纽约市的高楼大厦出现在了他们面前。他们终于到了美国！帕特里克在码头上，看到了一派繁忙的景象，完成了旅程的乘客们陆陆续续地从船上下来。帕特里克能感受到，这个发展中的新兴城市呈现出的勃勃生机和繁华喧嚣。这里跟都柏林几个世纪的沉静截然不同。

---

awkward *adj.* 难处理的   bustle *n.* 喧闹

◆ ATLANTIC CROSSING

"Why, Patrick, my boy!" he heard a familiar voice behind him. It was First Mate Thomas O'Brien, whom he had not seen for several days. Thomas came up to Patrick and put his hand on Patrick's shoulder.

Looking at Patrick's father, Thomas said, "You know, Mr. Kelly, none of us would be here in New York right now if it weren't for your son here." He looked down at Patrick and gave his shoulder a friendly shake. "What he did up on that mast in the storm was quite *courageous*. Quite *remarkable*."

"Thank you, sir," Patrick said, a little bit *embarrassed*.

"Well, we are all very proud of Patrick," Mr. Kelly said, looking *fondly* at his son. "And we are also very thankful to you and the rest of the crew of the *Donegal*," he continued. "Thanks to you, my family

"怎么了，帕特里克。孩子！"他听到身后传来一个熟悉的声音。是托马斯·奥布莱恩大副。他已经好几天没看到过大副了。托马斯走到帕特里克面前，把手放在了帕特里克的肩上。

看着帕特里克的父亲，托马斯说："您知道，凯利先生如果不是您儿子，我们所有人现在都不会站在纽约的土地上。"他低头看看帕特里克，友好地拍了一下他的肩膀说："他在暴风雨中，爬上了桅杆。这真的非常需要勇气，十分了不起。"

"谢谢您，先生。"帕特里克有点不好意思地说。

"我们都为帕特里克感到很骄傲。"凯利先生慈爱地看着自己的

courageous *adj.* 勇敢的 remarkable *adj.* 非凡的
embarrassed *adj.* 害羞的 fondly *adv.* 慈爱地

ADVENTURE TRIP I

now has a chance for a new life—a better life—here in America."

"I wish you all the luck in the world," Thomas answered. "And, Patrick, I hope to see you at the Harbor whenever the *Donegal* is in port. You *have the makings of* a fine sailor, and you're welcome on the deck of this ship any time."

Patrick smiled excitedly at this invitation and imagined his future, sailing the oceans of the world, but always returning to his family and to America, his new home.

儿子。"我们也很感谢您和多尼哥号上所有其他的船员。"他又说道,"多亏了你们,我和家人才有机会在美国这儿开始新的生活——美好的生活。"

"我祝你们好运。"托马斯答道,"帕特里克,我希望每次多尼哥号来到这个港口的时候,都能在这儿见到你。你具备优秀水手的潜质。欢迎你随时到这艘船上来。"

帕特里克对这个邀请感到很开心。他想象着自己的未来,在全世界的海上航行。不过,每次航行结束后,他都会回到家人身边,回到美国,他的新家。

---

have the makings of 具备了成为……的必要条件

07

Adventure in Bear Valley

"Going to California sure sounded like a grand idea when Ma and Pa were alive," Emily said in a low voice, the *hush* of the dark woods sending shivers down her *spine*.

Emily's brother Jess glanced *warily* at her as he picked up branches of firewood. "When Ma and Pa died, we didn't have any choice but to continue heading west."

Like many pioneers, their parents had died on the *perilous* trail

---

大熊谷历险记

"妈妈和爸爸活着的时候，去加利福尼亚真的是个好主意。"艾米丽轻声地说，漆黑阴森的森林使她感到脊背发直。

艾米丽的哥哥杰斯一边拾柴一边关心地看着她。"爸妈去世后，我们没有别的选择，只能继续向西走。"

跟许多拓荒者一样，他们的父母死在了去加利福尼亚的危险重重的

---

hush *n.* 鸦雀无声；寂静
warily *adv.* 小心地；谨慎地

spine *n.* 脊背
perilous *adj.* 危险的

ADVENTURE TRIP I

to California, and the Hutchinsons, a young pioneering couple, had taken them in. The four of them had traveled for days through the grandest, greenest mountains they had ever seen. They finally set up camp somewhere on the western slopes in California just as the sun's rays *faded* from the horizon of the late September sky.

"The Hutchinsons seem plenty nice enough," Emily said, reflecting on friendly Mrs. Hutchinson, a *timid* woman who spent most of her time in the *wagon*.

"We're not their family," Jess said shortly. "Don't tie to them just yet."

Their wagon train had left the plains of Missouri in April on the promise of hitting pay dirt in Sierra Nevada gold country by October. A couple weeks ago their wagon and a few others had *split* from the

---

山路上。哈钦森夫妇，一对年轻的开荒夫妻，收留了他们。他们四个已经在见过的最茂密最壮丽的大山中跋涉了好几天了。他们终于来到了加利福尼亚西坡的某个地方，他们决定在这里安营。这时，太阳已经落下了地平线，消失在这个九月末的天空中了。

"哈钦森夫妇人真的很好。"艾米丽说着在脑海中显现出友好的哈钦森夫人的形象——一个总是待在马车里的胆小的女人。

"我们不是他们的家人。"杰斯快言快语地说，"不要跟他们太纠缠在一起。"

他们四月份就从密苏里的平原出发了，预期在十月前抵达内华达山脉的黄金国家。几个星期前，在踏上了去亲戚家的路上，他们的马车和其他

---

fade v. 消失
wagon n. 马车

timid adj. 胆小的
split v. 分开

◆ ADVENTURE IN BEAR VALLEY

main group on a route that would lead them to *kin* who had already settled in California.

Being between hay and grass, Jess had signed on to be Mr. Hutchinson's *apprentice* after Ma and Pa passed. Mr. Hutchison, a rather bully blacksmith, planned to sell tools he made to *miners*. And where Jess went, Emily dutifully followed, helping Mrs. Hutchinson cook and do chores.

As they gathered more firewood, Emily heard *twigs* snap. A low growl came from a clump of trees to the left.

"Did you hear that?" Emily whispered urgently to Jess. "Let's head back. I don't like it out here," pleaded Emily as the shadows grew long and the forest turned dark as midnight.

"Afraid of some ol' boogeyman?" Jess teased gently. "Well, I

几辆马车离开了大队人马，他们的亲戚已经在加利福尼亚安顿下来了。

父母去世后，哈钦森先生发现了草丛中杰斯，收留他做学徒。哈钦森先生是个善良的铁匠，他打算把他打造的工具卖给那些矿工。杰斯去的地方，艾米丽自然要跟着，她帮哈钦森夫人做饭和做家务。

他们拾柴火的时候，艾米丽听到了树枝折断的声音。他们左边的树丛中有低低的叫声。

"你听见了吗？"艾米丽紧张地低声问杰斯。"我们回去吧，我不喜欢待在这里。"艾米丽恳求道。午夜的森林暗影浮动，漆黑一片。

"害怕有恶魔？"杰斯有点嘲弄地说道。"好吧，我想我们已经捡了

---

kin *n.* 亲戚
miner *n.* 矿工

apprentice *n.* 学徒
twig *n.* 树枝

ADVENTURE TRIP I

think we've got plenty of firewood anyway. Let's get out of here."

Walking back to camp, Emily couldn't help glancing over her shoulder every few steps.

"Just in time," Mr. Hutchinson said with a smile as they returned to camp. "I think the fire was about to *peter* out."

Jess *scowled*. It was just a harmless remark, but lately Jess was like a bear with a *sore* head around Mr. Hutchinson.

"Emily," Mrs. Hutchinson's voice interrupted her thoughts, "would you help me bake some biscuits?"

"I'd be glad to," Emily said. She walked over to the covered wagon—it stored everything they owned beneath its rounded *canvas* cover. Emily fetched the heavy iron skillet Mrs. Hutchinson used to make their meals.

足够多的柴火了，我们从这里出去吧。"

回营地的路上，艾米丽每走几步，就忍不住向后面望望。

"刚好来得及。"哈钦森先生看到他们回来后，笑着说。"我想，火快要灭了。"

杰斯皱了一下眉头。这句话没有恶意，但是杰斯后来像一个恼怒的熊一样，在哈钦森先生周围转来转去。

"艾米丽，"哈钦森夫人的声音打断了她的沉思，"你能帮我烤点饼干吗？"

"很乐意。"艾米丽说。她向篷车走去，他们所有的东西都放在它的

---

peter v. 逐渐减弱　　　　　　　　　　scowl v. 怒视
sore adj. 发怒的　　　　　　　　　　　canvas n. 帆布

ADVENTURE IN BEAR VALLEY

"*Campfire* biscuits again?" Jess said, "I'd give anything for a heapin' plate of Ma's biscuits."

Emily knew what he meant was that he'd give anything to have Ma back again.

Emily looked at Mr. and Mrs. Hutchinson. They'd both *winced* when Jess mentioned the biscuits. She hoped they didn't think Jess was criticizing Mrs. Hutchinson's cooking.

"Emily, when we get to Bear Valley," Mrs. Hutchinson said, "could you show me how to make your Ma's *recipe* for biscuits? I'm sure mine don't hold a candle to hers."

Before Emily could answer, Mr. Hutchinson said, "I have good news for you, dear. We just entered Bear Valley. We should be at your brother's homestead in a couple of days."

那个帆布圆篷下。艾米丽取出了哈钦森夫人用来做饭的沉重的长柄铁锅。

"又用篝火烤饼干了？"杰斯说，"我愿意用一切去换妈妈做的一盘饼干。"

艾米丽知道他的意思是如果能让妈妈活过来，他愿意付出一切。

艾米丽看向哈钦森夫妇，当杰斯提饼干的时候，他们俩的脸抽动了一下。她希望他们不要误会杰斯，以为他是在批评哈钦森夫人的厨艺。

"艾米丽，我们到大熊谷的时候，"哈钦森夫人说，"你能教我如何做你妈妈的秘制饼干吗？我想我做的跟她做的味道一定差远了。"

艾米丽还没来得及回答，哈钦森先生就说："亲爱的，告诉你个好消

---

campfire *n.* 篝火　　　　　　　　wince *v.* 皱起脸；皱眉蹙额
recipe *n.* 食谱

ADVENTURE TRIP 1

"Why do they call it Bear Valley?" Emily asked.

Mrs. Hutchinson gave her husband a look that said don't answer that, but he ignored it. "The children need to know the dangers in this *wilderness*, Elizabeth," he said to his wife.

He explained, "There are bears in these woods, big black bears, bigger *grizzly bears*, and even mountain lions. You need to be careful, and don't wander into the woods alone."

That night, Emily fell asleep quickly, dragged out by traveling and chores. She *tossed* and turned throughout the night as she dreamed of strange forest creatures.

The next morning, Emily awoke early to find a light frost had blanketed the ground. "I'll make *flapjacks*," she said to herself, wanting to surprise Jess and the Hutchinsons.

息。我们刚刚进入大熊谷。再有几天，我们就能到你哥哥家了。"

"人们为什么管这里叫大熊谷？"艾米丽问。

哈钦森夫人给丈夫一个眼神，让他不要回答，但是，她丈夫没理会。"孩子们需要了解这里的危险，伊丽莎白。"他对妻子说。

他解释道："在这儿的森林里有熊出没，大个的黑熊，这里的灰熊更大，甚至有狮子。你们必须小心，不要单独去树林里。"

那天晚上，艾米丽很快就睡着了，繁重的家务和长途跋涉把她累坏了。这个晚上她都在翻来覆去，因为她梦见了森林怪兽。

第二天早上，艾米丽醒得很早，她发现地面上笼罩着一层薄薄的雾。

---

wilderness *n.* 荒野
toss *v.* （使）摇摆

grizzly bear 灰熊
flapjack *n.* 煎饼

◆ ADVENTURE IN BEAR VALLEY

Emily *braided* her hair as the sun peeked over the mountains, burning off the frost. Emily was dying to change into a clean, pressed dress like her mother laid out for her on Sundays, but she'd have to wait until they reached the homestead.

The campfire *sputtered*, the flames all but dead. Emily leaned over intending to shake her brother awake to collect wood. But Jess looked so peaceful she couldn't bring herself to wake him. She wrapped up in a blanket and headed into the woods.

The morning was strangely silent, and a brisk *westerly* wind blew through the giant spruce trees. The sun had yet to penetrate the canopy of the evergreens. Emily shivered. She gathered wood, moving quickly. With her arms loaded with damp, dead wood, she turned back to camp. Again, she heard a low growl and her spine

---

"我要做煎饼。"她自言自语地说。她想给杰斯和哈钦森夫妇一个惊喜。

艾米丽梳头时，太阳照进了山里，雾散去了。艾米丽很想换上干净、笔挺的衣服，就像以前妈妈在星期天为她准备的那些衣服。但是，她必须等到他们安顿下来才能换衣服。

篝火发出噼啪的声音，火苗就要灭了。艾米丽俯下身，想叫醒哥哥，让他去捡柴火。可是，杰斯睡得很香，她不忍心叫醒他。她裹了一条毯子，向树林走去。

早晨的森林出奇的静，清新的风吹过巨大的云杉树，太阳还没穿过葱郁的树冠。艾米丽有些发抖。她快速地捡了一些柴火，抱着潮湿的柴火，

---

braid v. 将（头发）编成辫　　　　sputter v. 发噼啪声
westerly adj. 从西方吹来的

ADVENTURE TRIP 1

stiffened. The sound came closer.

Emily was too terrified to move. Her stomach tightened. She'd never see Jess again.

Just then Jess leaped from behind a giant *spruce* tree wearing a big *grin*.

Emily started: "I should feed you bark and dirt for that bosh, Jess Edward!"

Jess tried unsuccessfully to *stifle* his laughter.

"I was going to make you Ma's recipe for flapjacks," Emily taunted. "Now I've got second thoughts."

准备返回营地。她又一次听到了那个低低的叫声,她吓得直哆嗦。那个声音越来越近了。

艾米丽吓得都不能迈步了。她的心揪得紧紧的。她再也见不到杰斯了。

就在这时,杰斯从一棵巨大的云杉树后跳了出来,大声地笑了一下。

艾米丽开口说:"杰斯·爱德华,你这么胡闹,我要给你吃树皮和土!"

杰斯忍不住笑了出来。

"我本来打算给你做妈妈的秘制煎饼,"艾米丽逗着他说,"现在,我得好好想想了。"

---

stiffen v. 变僵硬
grin n. 咧嘴笑

spruce n. 云杉
stifle v. 阻止;抑制

◆ ADVENTURE IN BEAR VALLEY

Jess smiled, unapologetic. "Hold your horses, I was just joking. You know I love Ma's flapjacks."

Jess took some of the wood from Emily as she pinched his arm. Teasing like this made Jess's troubled face look almost happy.

When they returned, Mr. Hutchinson smiled and Emily smiled back. Jess *flinched*. Mr. Hutchinson was feeding the oxen. It was Jess's job to feed the animals in the morning and he thought Mr. Hutchinson might have a *blowup*. But Mr. Hutchinson held his tongue if he was angry.

"I'm making flapjacks," Emily explained.

Mr. Hutchinson grinned. "Elizabeth loves flapjacks," he said. "And so do I."

杰斯笑了,毫无悔改之意。"千万别,我只是在开玩笑。你知道我喜欢吃妈妈做的煎饼。"

杰斯从艾米丽手中接过了一些柴火,艾米丽掐了一下他的胳膊。这样的打闹使杰斯忧郁的脸舒展开了。

他们回来的时候,哈钦森先生向他们微笑,艾米丽也对他微笑。杰斯有点害怕。哈钦森先生正在喂牛。早晨喂牲口是杰斯的工作,他想,哈钦森先生也许会发火。但是,哈钦森先生生气时,是不会说话的。

"我要做煎饼。"艾米丽解释说。

哈钦森先生微笑着说:"伊丽莎白喜欢吃煎饼,我也喜欢。"

---

flinch *v.* 畏缩

blowup *n.* 发怒;发脾气

ADVENTURE TRIP 1

While Emily mixed *batter* for the flapjacks, Mr. Hutchinson went to wake his wife, but returned wearing a long frown, worry lines *creasing* his deeply tanned face.

"Elizabeth's got a fever. We'll have to stay here until she's feeling better," he said. "That means we should find more food and water. Our *provisions* won't last too much longer."

"I saw a stream back there," Jess offered. "We can refill our water canteens and maybe catch a few fish."

"I don't like to leave Elizabeth when she's feeling so poorly," Mr. Hutchinson said.

"I'll stay here and care for her," Emily volunteered, hoping to give Jess and Mr. Hutchinson much-needed time together.

艾米丽和面做煎饼时，哈钦森先生去叫妻子，但是他回来的时候，眉头紧锁，他深棕色的脸上现出忧愁的皱纹。

"伊丽莎白发烧了。我们得待在这，直到她好转。"他说，"那样的话，我们得找到充足的食物和水。我们的储备维持不了那么久。"

"我看到后面有一条小溪。"杰斯提议，"我们可以去那儿灌满水罐，也许还能抓到几条鱼。"

"我不想在伊丽莎白生病时，离开她。"哈钦森先生说。

"我会待在这儿，照顾她。"艾米丽自告奋勇地说。希望能给杰斯和哈钦森先生足够的待在一起的时间。

---

batter *n.* 面糊
provision *n.* 饮食供应

crease *v.* 使起皱纹

◆ ADVENTURE IN BEAR VALLEY

Mr. Hutchinson *reluctantly* agreed and gathered the canteens while Jess got the fishing *gear*.

Emily checked on Mrs. Hutchinson, who was awake and lying under a pile of blankets on a wooden pallet in the wagon.

"How are you feeling, Mrs. Hutchinson?" Emily inquired.

Mrs. Hutchinson gave her a weak smile. "Please, call me Elizabeth," she said. "You and Jess are family now."

Emily *cautiously* smiled back at her, uncertain of what to say.

"Would you like a cup of tea? Or maybe some flapjacks?" Emily said. " I covered them with a towel and kept them by the fire. They should still be warm."

哈钦森先生勉强同意了，去拿水罐。同时，杰斯去拿来了钓鱼用具。

艾米丽去看哈钦森夫人，她已经醒了，盖着毯子，躺在马车的木椅上。

"你感觉怎么样，哈钦森夫人？"艾米丽问。

哈钦森夫人勉强地挤出一个笑容。"请叫我伊丽莎白。"她说，"你和杰斯现在是家里人了。"

艾米丽拘束地向她笑笑，不知道该说什么。

"你想喝杯茶吗？或者来点煎饼怎么样？"艾米丽说，"我把它们放在火上了，用毛巾盖着，应该不会凉。"

---

reluctantly　*adv.*　不情愿地；勉强地　　　　　　　　gear　*n.*　用具；设备
cautiously　*adv.*　小心地

ADVENTURE TRIP I

Elizabeth nodded gratefully.

Emily hurried down from the wagon to make tea and get the flapjacks. As she approached the fire, she stopped dead in her *tracks*. There in the campsite stood a rather small bear *gulping* down Elizabeth's flapjacks. Emily's mind raced, but she was frozen to the spot. She stared at the bear for a few *agonizingly* slow seconds, trying to remember everything her Pa had taught her about wild animals.

Emily realized the animal must have been attracted to the camp by the smell of food. She tried to remember everything she'd ever been told about bears, but her mind went blank.

The young grizzly hadn't noticed her yet, but Emily knew a *cub* in

伊丽莎白感激地点点头。

艾米丽赶紧下了马车，去沏茶，取煎饼。来到火边时，她突然停住了脚步。营地里有一只小熊在吃着伊丽莎白的煎饼。艾米丽的心怦怦直跳，完全僵在了那里。她盯了那只熊仅仅几秒钟，试着回想爸爸教给她的关于野生动物的所有知识。

艾米丽意识到一定是食物的味道把这只熊吸引到营地来了。她试着记起所有关于熊的知识，但是，她的脑子一片空白。

这只小灰熊还没注意到她，但是，艾米丽知道营地里的小熊意味着熊

track *n.* 足迹
agonizingly *adv.* 极其

gulp *v.* 狼吞虎咽地吃
cub *n.* 幼兽

◆ ADVENTURE IN BEAR VALLEY

ADVENTURE TRIP 1

camp meant the mother was most likely *lurking* nearby. She needed to get the cub out of there and fast—but how?

Emily backed away slowly. She needed to get back to the wagon before Elizabeth came out to see what was taking so long. Everything inside her wanted to run, but somehow she knew that was the worst thing to do. The bear would probably think of her as fresh food if she ran. She slowly backed away. She froze when the bear cub suddenly lifted its head and *sniffed* the air, exposing its sharp, sharp teeth.

妈妈可能就在附近。她需要快点把小熊弄走，可是，要怎么才能弄走呢？
　　艾米丽慢慢地向后退，她必须尽快回到马车，以免伊丽莎白出来，察看她为什么会耽搁这么久。她心里非常想跑，但是，她知道那样会带来最坏的结果。如果她跑，熊可能会以为她是猎物。她慢慢地向后挪动着身体。那只小熊突然抬起头，用鼻子在空气中嗅了嗅，露出了非常锋利的牙齿，她赶紧一动不动地站在那里。

lurk *v.* 潜伏　　　　　　　　　　　　　　　　sniff *v.* 嗅；闻

◆ ADVENTURE IN BEAR VALLEY

Emily didn't move and the cub went back to *foraging* for food. Emily had an idea, but she had to get back to the wagon. She forced herself to *gingerly* walk the last few steps to the wagon and climbed in, breathing hard.

"Emily, what's wrong?" Elizabeth said, "Your face is as white as a sheet."

"There's a bear cub outside," Emily said, "And its mom is probably close by."

"What should we do?" Elizabeth said.

"I have an idea," Emily said, as she peeked out of the wagon.

艾米丽没敢动，那只小熊又回去吃食了。艾米丽有了主意，但是，她得回到马车里。她小心翼翼地挪动了最后几步，爬进了马车，用力地喘着气。

"艾米丽，怎么了？"伊丽莎白说，"你的脸色怎么这么苍白。"

"外面有个小熊。"艾米丽说，"它的妈妈也许就在附近。"

"我们该怎么办？"伊丽莎白说。

"我有个主意。"伊丽莎白说着偷偷地向马车外面看去。眼前的景象

---

forage *v.* 觅（食）   gingerly *adv.* 谨慎地

ADVENTURE TRIP I

What she saw outside made her sick with fear. A second bear had joined the cub, and this one was huge, with *frighteningly* large *claws* and teeth.

"Oh, no," she breathed, but Elizabeth heard her.

"What is it?" she asked *anxiously*.

"The mama bear is here," Emily said, "Now I don't know if my idea will work."

She knew Mr. Hutchinson and Jess wouldn't be back at camp for hours, and they had the rifle. Emily had promised Mr. Hutchinson that she would take care of Elizabeth.

令她毛骨悚然。小熊的旁边又来了一大熊，长着可怕的大爪子和牙齿。

"哦，不。"她低声说，但是，伊丽莎白听见了她的话。

"怎么了？"她焦急地问。

"熊妈妈来了。"艾米丽说，"现在，我不知道我的主意会不会有用了。"

她知道哈钦森先生和杰斯在几个小时内都不会回来，他们拿走了来复枪。艾米丽向哈钦森先生保证她会照顾好伊丽莎白。

---

frighteningly *adv.* 令人恐惧地
anxiously *adv.* 焦急地

claw *n.* 爪子

◆ ADVENTURE IN BEAR VALLEY

Elizabeth got up from her pallet, pale and shaky, but *determined*. "I'll help. Tell me what you want me to do."

Emily said, "We'll need the pots and pans. Help me take them down."

They lifted the pots and pans down from where they hung on hooks along the wagon's frame.

"I'm scared," Emily *admitted*.

Elizabeth said: "Me, too. But we can do this together."

They smiled warily at each other. When Elizabeth reached over and gave her a quick hug, Emily felt a warm *glow*.

伊丽莎白从椅子上站起来，面色苍白，浑身发抖，但却坚定地说："我来帮你。告诉我做什么。"

艾米丽说："我们需要锅和盆，帮我把它们拿下来。"

她们从马车架子上的钩子上，取下锅和盆。

"我很害怕。"艾米丽承认说。

伊丽莎白说："我也是。不过，我们可以一起做。"

她们互相笑了一下。这时，伊丽莎白伸出手，迅速地给了她一个拥抱。艾米丽心中涌出了一股暖流。

---

determined *adj.* 坚定的
glow *n.* 喜悦；满足的心情

admit *v.* 承认

ADVENTURE TRIP 1

"Now what?" Elizabeth said.

"Now we bang the pots and pans as loudly as we can," Emily said. "My Pa told me once that bears don't like loud noises. On the count of three; one, two, three!"

They beat the pots and pans loudly and yelled until they were *hoarse*. Finally, they stopped, exhausted.

Emily and Elizabeth peeked out of the wagon to the quiet campsite.

"I don't see anything, do you?" Elizabeth asked.

Emily answered, "No, I think they're gone."

"现在，做什么？"伊丽莎白说。

"现在我们用力地敲打这些锅和盆。"艾米丽说，"爸爸曾经告诉过我，熊不喜欢噪音。她数着：一，二，三！"

她们使劲敲打锅和盆，高声叫喊，直到嗓子都叫哑了。最后，她们停下了，疲惫不堪。

艾米丽和伊丽莎白偷偷地从马车向外面望去，看见了安静的营地。

"我什么也没看见，你呢？"伊丽莎白问。

艾米丽回答："没有，它们走了。"

---

hoarse *adj.* 嘶哑的

◆ ADVENTURE IN BEAR VALLEY

The two of them remained in the wagon for a long time after that just to be sure, but there was no sign of the bears.

Finally, Emily said. "Would you like a cup of tea now?"

"Yes, please, but I think I'll skip the flapjacks." Elizabeth said.

They looked at each other and *collapsed* into *gales of laughter*, relieved that the danger had passed. They left the protection of the wagon, confident that they had *chased* the bears away.

"Wait!" Emily said. She ran to the wagon and came back carrying pots and pans.

"Just in case," she said, handing two pans to Elizabeth.

她们俩在马车里待了很久，想确定一下。但是，没有任何熊的踪迹。

最后，艾米丽说："你想喝杯茶吗，现在？"

"好的。不过，我想我就不要煎饼了。"伊丽莎白说。

她们互相看了看，一下子笑了出来，危险已经过去了，她们都松了口气。她们下了马车，很确信熊已经被她们赶走了。

"等等！"艾米丽说着跑向马车，取出了锅和盆。

"以防万一。"她说着递给伊丽莎白两个锅。

---

collapse *v.* （突然）瓦解　　　　gales of laughter 一阵（阵）大笑声
chase *v.* 追赶

ADVENTURE TRIP I

Suddenly, they heard a twig *snap* and a sound coming toward them.

They screamed as loudly as they could and banged on their pots and pans.

When Mr. Hutchinson and Jess walked into view, they were carrying fishing poles and a line of *trout*. They also had *perplexed* looks on their faces.

"Elizabeth, what in the world are you doing up?" Mr. Hutchinson asked. "What's going on?"

Jess asked, "Emily, are you all right?"

突然,她们听到了树枝折断的声音,还有一个声音离她们越来越近。
她们高声喊叫,使劲地敲打着锅和盆。
这时候,她们看见了哈钦森先生和杰斯,他们拿着渔竿和一串鱼。他们脸上带着困惑的表情。
"伊丽莎白,你们到底在干什么?"哈钦森先生问,"怎么回事?"
杰斯问:"艾米丽,你还好吗?"

---

snap *v.* (使)啪的一声绷断　　　　　　　　　　trout *n.* 鳟鱼
perplexed *adj.* 困惑的

◆ ADVENTURE IN BEAR VALLEY

"We thought you were the bears," Emily explained.

"Oh that's rich, Em!" Jess said not believing bears had come and he had missed it.

"No, it's true, we had a bit of a fuss with a mother and her cub," Mrs. Hutchinson replied.

"What mother and cub?" Mr. Hutchinson worriedly asked.

Elizabeth and Emily shared the rest of their *dreadfully* exciting adventure as Jess and Mr. Hutchinson admired their bravery.

"我们以为你们是熊。"艾米丽解释道。

"哦,还有这事!"杰斯说道。他不相信他不在的时候,熊来过了。

"是真的。我们遇到了一个熊妈妈和熊宝宝。"哈钦森夫人回答。

"什么熊妈妈和熊宝宝?"哈钦森先生担心地问。

伊丽莎白和艾米丽讲述了她们非常刺激的冒险经历,杰斯和哈钦森先生很敬佩她们的勇气。

dreadfully *adv.* 极其;非常